Learning
Resource Centre

Stockton
Riverside College

618·92

NWEB 8

BEHAVIOUR PROBLEMS IN CHILDREN: Orthodox and Paradox in Therapy

his book is to be returned on or before
the last date stamped below

and Community Services
Stockton-Billingham Technical College
The Causeway, Billingham, Cleveland, TS23 2DB.

D1634364

BEHAVIOUR PROBLEMS IN CHILDREN: Orthodox and Paradox in Therapy

Robert Wilkins MB MRCP MRCPsych.

Illustrations by Penny Loudon

Heinemann Nursing

Heinemann Nursing
An imprint of Heinemann Professional Publishing Ltd
Halley Court, Jordan Hill, Oxford OX2 8EJ

OXFORD LONDON SINGAPORE NAIROBI IBADAN
KINGSTON

First published 1989

© Robert Wilkins 1989

British Library Cataloguing in Publication Data

Wilkins, Robert
    Behaviour problems in children.
    1. Children. Behaviour therapy
    I. Title
    618.92'89142
ISBN 0 433 00072 4

Learning
Resource Centre
Stockton
Riverside College

618.92

Typeset by Graphicraft Typesetters Ltd, Hong Kong
Printed and bound in Great Britain by
Biddles Ltd, Guildford and King's Lynn

Contents

Dedicated to the memory of my parents

Preface

In social situations it is not uncommon for people to distance themselves from me as soon as they discover that I am a psychiatrist. When I qualify my job by saying that I am a *child and adolescent* psychiatrist I soon regain acceptance – I am then frequently asked my opinion and advice concerning the atrocious behaviour of a friend's child. Such impromptu consultations have convinced me that there is a great interest among adults about why children behave as they do, and how such behaviour can be changed.

This book has been written as an introduction to behaviour modification for psychiatric nurses and all other professionals whose jobs frequently entail them giving advice to parents about children's problem behaviours. It has eschewed jargon as far as possible and thus may be readily understood by interested parents. It is essentially a practical guide distilled from experience gained in the settings of a child guidance clinic and a family and young persons unit. Although most of the book is given over to orthodox approaches used in behaviour modification, a substantial portion considers more unusual and paradoxical therapies.

Too many books about behaviour modification appear to offer therapists infallible methods. I sincerely hope that this book does not imply that success can always be guaranteed since I have endeavoured at all times to highlight the common pitfalls in the application of behaviour modification techniques and ways in which they may be overcome.

Many of the problem behaviours discussed in this book, e.g. temper tantrums, can be tackled by a variety of therapeutic approaches. For this reason I suggest that all the possible alternative strategies should be considered before a choice is made about the treatment of any particular behaviour. Both the behaviour itself and the personality of the child or young person displaying that behaviour must be assessed before embarking upon a treatment programme.

Note: The masculine pronoun 'he' has been used when referring to the child. This is for convenience and clarity and does not reflect a preference for either sex.

1
First principles

'Thankfully children are not alike and mine are very different to yours.'

A parent's response to this is often:

> Oh God! He's starting off by saying his kids are different from mine. He probably has children who always do as they are told, never answer back or get into trouble, don't swear, and simply adore cabbage and asparagus. I bet he's never had to thump them in his life. He probably sees my kids as complete horrors who I'm ashamed of most of the time because they're always out of control and never do or say anything nice. I bet he's going to say it's all my fault, that I should reason with them instead of hitting them, and then he'll go on and talk down to me as if I were an incompetent cretin. I'd like him to have my children for just one week....

Authors of self-help books must have nightmares thinking how their advice may backfire on them. What happens to the self-esteem when a writer of a sex manual becomes suddenly impotent; when the garage of a do-it-yourself expert falls down; or when a fitness fanatic drops dead in his thirties? Such are my own misgivings when I think that this book purports to advise therapists on how to alter children's behaviour, especially when I remember how the antics of my own children frequently cause me severe chest pain and leave me thinking that it would have been a lot easier to have become a monk.

Nevertheless, for most of the time, like most other people's children, mine behave tolerably well and in a manner that I and my wife find acceptable. But tolerance is a two-way process: at times my children are ungrateful, egocentric, defiant and treat the home as if it were a hotel; just as often, I am reliably informed by my teenage offspring, I appear to them as an out-of-touch, repressive, narrow-minded killjoy whose sole purpose is to stop them having fun.

The problem of consistency

It is undeniable that parental inconsistency is at the root of many behavioural problems seen in children, and if parents were magically to become totally consistent then many of these problems would evaporate. Realistically, most of us would find such consistency unattainable. We are all of us different people on different days – even from hour to hour during the same day. A child who wants a sweet might be persuaded that he can't have one because it is 5.30 and too close to his mealtime. What will greatly confuse him is the fact that he was given a sweet at 5.30 yesterday. If he is old enough to point this inconsistency out to his mother, it is quite likely that he will be told sharply: 'That was yesterday!' Inconsistency is a very human failing.

Inconsistency, and its propensity to produce bad behaviour, starts almost from the day one is born. A baby is extremely limited in what he can do. He is dependent on other people for his every need. When he is hungry he cries and this is his way of telling his mother that he wants food. Very soon he comes to associate the fact that, within a short time of starting to cry, a bottleful of sweet warm milk is put in his mouth. Everything is fine just so long as mother drops whatever she is doing and hot-foots it immediately to pander to his every need. A generation of infants spent their babyhood having their expectation of immediate gratification met by mothers who had been told by one Dr Benjamin Spock that feeding on demand was the way to bring up children. That worked fine for mothers who had nothing better to do than to have their whole lives geared to the whims of their children. For the rest, those parents whose baby could not always take precedence over everything else, it was inevitable that inconsistent maternal responses would affect the child's perception of the world.

Battle commences the very first time a baby's wishes are not instantly gratified. It is the first example of inconsistency on his mother's part – and precisely how this situation is resolved can affect the behaviour of the child through babyhood, infancy, adolescence and into adulthood. When a baby, unused to delay of any kind, does not quickly see his mother's smiling face, bottle ready in hand, he becomes confused. Perhaps she did not hear. He cries louder. If mother can then come swiftly down a ladder or from the loo, and if she can show her distress at keeping her little prince waiting, then she might be reluctantly forgiven – provided she never does it again.

It would be a pity to labour the point since most babies and their parents come to a compromise about issues such as feeding and changing times, and offspring soon begin to accept that the world does not revolve around their oral and anal needs. The children are learning that adults sometimes will do as they are told – but sometimes they will not; that sometimes parents will get angry at a certain behaviour while at other times they will accept the same behaviour without protest. To a great extent infancy is the time when a child learns what things are *never* acceptable to either his father or mother, what things are *sometimes* acceptable and sometimes not, and what things he might be able to get away with sometimes with father and sometimes with mother.

The result of this process varies from child to child and from parent to parent. For those ultra-rigid parents who are always consistent and who never make exceptions to the rules then at least the children always know where they stand. Whether this makes for harmonious living is another matter. For the larger group of parents, rules are more flexible and negotiable, and each side gets its own way some of the time – most often the parents, but occasionally the children. In this 'ideal' set-up it is to be hoped that the children do not regard getting their own way as a reflection of parental weakness.

Major problems arise when children become so used to getting their own way that their parents' lives are subjugated to the children's instant gratification. These are parents who either give in immediately or after a very feeble attempt to exercise their authority. Even though such parents may realize that a child is being hopelessly spoilt, they still cannot bring themselves to deny him anything. This book is intended to teach therapists to help such parents take stock of their situation, decide whether they really want to have more control over their children's behaviour, and look at ways, both orthodox and more unusual, in which such control can be gained. None of the methods in this book is guaranteed to be successful; you will probably have tried many of them already; some may strike you as callous or unfeeling.

What is 'normal' behaviour?

There is no such thing as normal behaviour. Just as some people are tall and others are fat, some behave in one way and others in another. Of course there are some forms of behaviour which most people would agree are unacceptable in a civilized society, but even these differ from time to time and from country to country. Moses gave the Israelites ten commandments for acceptable behaviour, most of which, though by no means all, would be thought appropriate today.

The same principle applies to families. Whilst most of us would agree that it is preferable that children do not lie, steal or set fires, there would probably be less unanimity about boisterousness, bullying (which might be connoted as 'sticking up for yourself in a cruel world') or swearing. Each family must set its own standards. Although a neighbour's child may always do as he is told immediately and never answer back, it does not necessarily follow that this is the behaviour you would wish to see in your own child – what about that independent streak you always hoped a child of yours would possess? Expectations about your child's behaviour should be your own and not those of your sister, mother-in-law or vicar – and least of all, therapists or authors of self-help books such as this!

Bad behaviour is not an absolute concept

Parental tolerance of a child's behaviour may vary: many adults will put up with certain behaviours within the home that they would not tolerate outside – such behaviour, bad as it may be, is confined within the family. Paul may be horrendous to live with, but the fact that butter would not melt in his mouth when he goes to school, or goes shopping with mother, or goes to visit granny, makes his parents inclined to be grateful that things are not a lot worse and to hope fervently that he will become more civilized as he grows older. Friends or neighbours who drop in for tea might be appalled at the mayhem, but a mother may decide that it is really none of their business and that they can always exercise their option to have tea somewhere else. If 'doormat' mothers and fathers are willing to be trodden on by their children then should not the rest of us respect their wishes and refrain from interfering? 'He wouldn't get away with that if he was my son' may be viewed as quite unhelpful if he is not your son and you are not his parent.

But most people agree that the situation changes fundamentally when 'bad' behaviour spills out of the home and starts to affect people outside the family. As soon as a child's behaviour starts to impinge upon others then it is no longer one's private business. It is at this time that the opinions of outsiders gain a legitimacy. The first outsiders likely to complain are the teachers in a playgroup or infant school. Some parents begin to feel persecuted for the trouble their children are causing and may resent the fact that they are criticized for behaviour that they themselves readily accept. Nevertheless, social pressures can be very strong and often mark the point when parents seek help.

What are the risks of bad behaviour?

Bad behaviour, even if initially confined to the home, generally has long-term risks:

1. Other children, both in the family and, more importantly, outside the family, will often be unwilling to play with someone who is, say, aggressive and always wants his own way. Consequently a child may become known as a bully, or other parents may refuse to let their children play with him. The risk is that he will end up friendless – or else those friends he does have are only friendly through fear.
2. Relatives or visitors may start to criticize a child's conduct and suggest that 'there may be something wrong with him'. They might tap their temples and say knowingly: 'He's a bit...you know'. A parent might begin to think that the child may be 'mad' and they may cast around the family – usually the other side of the family – for people he takes after.
3. Arguments between parents often start with disagreements

about how to manage children. If one parent thinks that the other is too soft, or if one thinks the other never backs her up in matters of discipline, then this is often the beginning of deep resentments or full-blown rows that may end in violence, injury or divorce. Short of divorce, a mother may feel herself helpless or hopeless and become suicidally depressed.

4. Whilst the majority of children with behavioural problems do grow out of them and become more socially acceptable, it is nevertheless still a fact that a badly behaved child is more likely to grow into a badly behaved adult. Aggressive and self-centred children who are used to getting their own way will expect immediate gratification in adult life and become bitter, angry and hostile when it does not happen.

Aggressive and antisocial behaviour in childhood is especially worrying for adult development if:

a. it starts early.
b. it spills out of the home and into the community.
c. it happens frequently.
d. it results in poor relationships with other children of the same age.

Behaviour and personality

A lot of nonsense is talked about behaviour and personality. What is personality? Personality is what makes me different from you, and what makes you different from everyone else. If you could analyse your personality in much the same way as a chemist analyses a mixture of substances, the computer print-out might include such descriptions as easy-going, enjoys a joke, easily upset by Third World problems, intolerant of hypocrisy, friendly, hard-working and so on. You are a unique person and are made up of these attributes in various proportions. Someone else might have a very different personality – he might be aggressive, spiteful, greedy, self-centred and humourless.

Now a child who is used to getting his own way and creates mayhem when he does not get it is selfish and aggressive, and these two adjectives describe part of his personality. It is what makes him different from his sister. It may now become apparent why it is illogical for a parent to say: 'I want him to be a nicer person and do as I tell him, but I don't want to change his personality'. His defiance is part of his personality, the very part of his personality that you *do* want to change. The other parts of his personality, the bits that include kindness to animals, being good at sport or helping his father clean the car, are those parts you want to keep.

Parents who want their children's behaviour to change are actually asking for a personality change – they want to substitute unacceptable parts of personality with nicer parts. That is a perfectly reasonable thing to want to do and is in no way similar to meddling with children's brains in some Frankenstein-like fashion.

When is a problem a problem?

The simple answer is 'when the parents can agree that it is a problem'. Unfortunately this is not always as easy as it sounds and although parents may *appear* to agree, deep down they may believe one thing and say the opposite. When one parent secretly does not want the behaviour of a child to alter, it is small wonder that things do not change. Indeed, matters often get very much worse.

One of the forms of bad behaviour which most frequently comes to the attention of therapists is the young boy, say five years old, who is defiant and aggressive to his mother but will do things instantly when his father asks him to. In most cases father is easily and genuinely convinced that such an attitude towards mother is not healthy and that his son will grow up to treat all females in a similar way, including his future wife. In instances like this it is easy to get agreement on what the problem is and to motivate father to stand by his wife as they both attempt to get more reasonable and civilized behaviour from their child.

The outcome then depends on consistency and high motivation. When a boy's behaviour does not change, despite the parents appearing to do all the right things, the reason for the failure often lies in unspoken motives – usually held by father – for the defiant behaviour to continue. What possible reason could a father have for wanting such tyranny to continue? Your guess is as good as mine, but this would be mine:

> Father and mother have a poor marriage and he is resentful about her always nagging him and telling him what to do. Father was always a bit of a wimp and secretly admires his son for being much more manly than *he* ever was and for putting women in their place. He especially relishes the way his wife does not seem able to deal with their son and does his best to encourage his son's behaviour in covert, non-verbal ways such as smiling behind his wife's back.

The motivation of such a father to change his son's behaviour is non-existent, despite what he says, and it is small wonder that the boy continues to treat his mother badly. The child has become an innocent pawn in a game of marital politics.

Why does he do it?

Many parents just cannot understand why a child chooses to behave badly when it would be so much better for all concerned if he behaved in a reasonable way. Perhaps the best way to explain what might be going on is by giving an example. If four-year-old Tom is used to being waited on hand and foot by his mother he is certainly not going to appreciate it if one day mother asks him to put his toys away. He will, in all probability, pretend he did not hear and carry on oblivious. Often mother will 'tut-tut' at this point and good-naturedly set about tidying away the toys herself.

Suppose that mother has just had an earful from a friend about how she allows Tom to 'get away with murder', and how 'it isn't going to do him any good when he goes to school'. Mother's resentment about being criticized gives way to a feeling that her friend is probably right, and so she resolves that things must change. Tom is not at all impressed and totally ignores his mother's request. She asks again, louder and more firmly than before. He does not even bother to look up. Mother, unsure of what to do next, starts to shout and get angry. There are a number of things that can happen now.

When the chips are down

The best outcome would be for Tom suddenly to get the message that things have changed, and that if they are not to get an awful lot worse, he had better clear away his toys as fast as possible. If this, the best of all possible solutions, was to happen, then mother would wait until the toys had been put away and say: 'Well done, Tom. Just for that, how about an icecream after tea?' Tom will recognize that tidying away toys is a small price to pay for an icecream and he will willingly comply the next time. Tom has been given a reward for his good behaviour, and that reward, often known in the trade as a *reinforcer*, means that he is more likely to tidy away his toys more quickly next time if he thinks he will get an icecream.

But what if things do not work out so well? Say, for instance, that Tom is unimpressed by promises of icecream and is certainly not moved to clear away his toys in order to get one. Mother has to decide whether she wants a showdown. Let us suppose that she does and she pulls Tom away from what he is doing and threatens all manner of punishments if he does not do as he is told. In most houses this would have a fairly predictable outcome. The boy would realize he was no match for an angry mum, and he would tidy up 'just this once'. Alternatively Tom could relish a battle of wills and raise the stakes by shouting back just as loudly. It then becomes a battle royal and the one who wins is likely to continue to win in the future.

Many mothers, faced by a screaming child, will quickly wave the white flag and surrender unconditionally. There are a number of reasons given by mothers to explain their capitulation. Here are some:

1.   She was afraid she would hurt him.
2.   She was afraid he would hurt her.
3.   She was afraid of what the neighbours might think.
4.   He would wake up the baby or he would wake up dad who is on night shift.
5.   He would have made a mess of the job anyway.

and perhaps the most common reason of all:

6.   Anything for a peaceful life.

Now I can just feel some parents begin to bristle with anger. 'It's all very well for so-called experts to sit in their offices and spout about what we should do – they don't have to put up with unfriendly neighbours/sleeping babies/four-year-old sons with a punch like a flat iron.' And it is true – most therapists do not have any of these problems. But it is just as true that whatever the final reason for Tom not clearing away his toys, he will see it as a victory and will be equally as determined not to clear up in the future. As he grows through childhood, the odds will go even more in his favour, since he will grow bigger, more muscular and more physically powerful. He will also inevitably become the role model for his younger brothers and sisters who will mimic his behaviour.

Now here is the point: Tom behaves badly *because it suits him to do so.*

So why change?

For Tom to change his attitude he must become convinced that there is something in it for him. This reward could be icecream or it could be the pleasure he gets from pleasing his mother, or it could be that he was bright enough to know that if he did not do it then something unpleasant would happen to him. Whatever the pay-off for Tom, he is unlikely to change unless the advantages of doing something outweigh the disadvantages. Changing someone's behaviour is all about persuading people that there is some advantage in it for them. Why else would anyone want to change?

When a smack is reward in itself

What parents might not understand so readily is the reason why a child continues to behave in an unacceptable way even when he knows it may result in severe punishment. Surely a smack is no reward?

The answer in most cases is that the child simply wants attention from a parent, and he is not fussy whether that attention takes the form of a kiss or a clout. He wants to be recognized as being there, even if it only serves to focus anger upon himself. It is easier to accept this explanation of bad behaviour in families where the father or mother, or both, seem to take virtually no interest in the children at all, and where parents seem to be oblivious to their children. In such families perhaps the only way a child can announce his presence is by deliberately provoking a parent into violence.

But people find it more difficult to accept this explanation in families where, on the surface, the needs of the child are always in the parents' minds. The problem is that in this type of family, often goal-seeking, middle-class environments, the material and intellectual needs of the child might be met, but not his emotional ones. He may have every computer toy and electronic gadget on the market but he could be missing the interest or companionship of a mother who is trying desperately to hold down a part-time job, or a father who comes home late and is away most weekends. In such situations the only way that a child may call attention to himself is by indulging in bad behaviour – stealing, lying, cruelty to the cat. Any attention is better than none at all.

Why it is better not to try at all than to go off half-cock

Imagine that Joe and Joan had a ballpoint pen each. Joe's stopped writing and no matter how much he tried no ink appeared. Joan's pen also stopped writing, but by shaking it she was able to get it to write again. A little while later, Joan's pen dries up again, but she is able to get it writing for a second time.
Question: Who is likely to throw their pen away first?

Answer: Joe. The reason is that Joe quickly realizes that his pen has totally run out of ink and that it is pointless hoping that it will ever write again. Joan, on the other hand, is far from convinced that her pen has packed up since with a little bit of coaxing she can get it to write again.

The similarity with trying to change a child's behaviour is not difficult to see and highlights the importance of motivation in increasing the likelihood of success. If you decide once and for all, come what may, that a certain behaviour will never again be tolerated, then before long most children will accept the inevitable and realize that whatever opposition they show will not have the slightest effect in lessening your determination. The old regime is over, the pen is dry.

Alternatively, if a child sees that by putting up a vigorous resistance he will manage to get his own way as often as you get yours, then he is obviously less likely to be persuaded to change. With a bit of coaxing he thinks he stands a good chance of winning and so he will fight to the bitter end. The pen is not dry.

But what about food additives?

It is not the intention of this book to spend much time on the effects of junk food on behaviour – usually taken to imply a worsening of aggression and overactivity. Neither is it the intention to claim that there is no link between what we eat and how we behave: after all, someone once said: 'We are what we eat'. But the fact remains that no definite foods have been shown to be responsible for bad behaviour in children.

The best advice to give to parents who bring up the subject of diet and behaviour is that they should seek expert advice on those substances thought most likely to be responsible. Then they must try their best to eliminate the substance, and all foods containing that substance, from the child's diet. The suspect foods must be omitted for about a month and the effects upon behaviour noted as accurately as possible. If there is no appreciable effect then it is pointless going to the trouble of carrying on any longer. That particular food is allowed back in the family diet and another one is chosen to be omitted for the following month. This is a very arduous procedure and one that can be very expensive in both time and money.

A major problem seems to be that foods thought to bring on aggressive behaviour or overactivity are the very ones that children like most – hamburgers, cola, chocolate and so on. It is therefore very difficult to be sure that children are not managing to obtain secret supplies, often bought with pocket money or else inadvertently given by relatives or friends.

If parents come saying that their child's behaviour greatly improved when they cut out cola, then everyone is happy – except, perhaps, the child. But one must caution against over-optimism, especially in the early days of enthusiasm for a new diet. A therapist may wisely suggest that diet may not be the whole answer, especially if, after obtaining a detailed description of the behaviour and the circumstances in which that behaviour usually arises, it is obvious that there are other, more likely reasons, why a child behaves as badly as he does.

Most therapists are unimpressed by claims of *long-lasting* improvement in behaviour as a result of a change in a child's diet, but feel it would be a gross impertinence to try to persuade parents not to attempt dietary manipulation.

Conclusion

Behaviour modification is hard work for the parents and calls for much motivation, consistency and *love*.

2

The spectrum of behaviour problems in childhood

What types of problems are there?

Pyschiatrists and psychologists often classify children's problems into behavioural and emotional categories. The emotional category includes anxiety and depression – feelings which all of us have experienced at some time or other. Although specific treatment for these fall outside the scope of this book, they can often be the cause of problem *behaviours*. In fact, people who set out to change or modify a child's behaviour are often accused of paying little or no attention to any underlying *emotional* cause for the problem. To this charge behaviour modification therapists must often plead guilty.

Aggressive behaviours and absent fathers

As an example of how an emotional factor may be the cause of a behavioural problem, consider a seven-year-old boy who defies his mother and acts in an aggressive and dangerous way to his younger sister. If, after an assessment, it is thought that the lad is trying to punish his mother for allowing his father to go off with another woman, some doctors would think that more progress is likely to be made if the question of the absent father is addressed – even though the father may have no interest in the boy and no intention of ever returning home.

It often happens that parents who have separated still share a natural concern about their children's welfare, and many children who realize this are tempted to behave badly in the hope that it will bring the parents back together again. Unfortunately this is usually a forlorn hope. Therapists in behaviour modification would maintain that the boy's behaviour must change first and foremost, before something dangerous happens. The emotional problems concerned with father's absence can be dealt with separately and at a later time.

Sibling rivalry

Another example may be an aggressive four-year-old girl (just for a change!) whose unfriendly and malicious attitude to a baby brother may have its roots in understandable jealousy. While possible causes for the behaviour must be borne in mind, the urgent priority is to persuade the girl that such dangerous behaviour will not be tolerated and will always be punished. (If a quiver goes down your spine at the very mention of 'punishment', rest assured that physical violence is not being advocated. A more detailed discussion of the different forms of punishment will be found later in the book.) Once again an emotional root of a problem takes second place to a more immediate need to alter behaviour.

For the reasons given above, it is intended that this book will generally confine itself to consideration of behavioural problems and avoid emotional ones. Behavioural problems seen in a psychiatric setting include:

1. The child who is always 'on the go'.
2. The child who is destructive.
3. The child who will not do as he is told.
4. The child who is aggressive or spiteful to other children.
5. The child who will not eat.
6. The child who will not go to bed.
7. The child who refuses to go to school.
8. The child who persists in coming into the parental bed.
9. The child who lies or steals.

Less common, but more serious problems include children who run away from home and those who set fires.

Are parents to blame?

The honest answer to this frequently asked question is that it is difficult to know who to blame if not the parents. But that is not meant to imply that anyone else would have necessarily done any better given the same circumstances. The point is that if the parents can see that it was their lack of clear boundaries that allowed a child to get away with something he should not have got away with, then it is easier to persuade the parents that the *remedy* also lies in their hands. If, in an attempt to spare the parents' feelings, the impression is given that the fault lies with the child, then the impetus of the parents to change things may be less sustained. They may also be less vigilant if they think that the cause is in the child's genes, and therefore unchangeable.

Some things are more obviously the parents' responsibility than the child's. Getting into the parental bed is the obvious example. If a child grows up getting his own way at all times and this results in difficulties getting him to bed, or getting him up, or getting him to do as he is told, again it is the parents' lack of boundaries which is probably responsible.

Other behavioural problems are less obviously the parents' fault, such as stealing or setting fires, unless, after an assessment, it is deemed that such behaviours are the result of attempts on the child's part to get attention from uninterested parents.

The isolated nuclear family

You might think it strange that in this day and age, with all the books available to tell parents how to bring up children, problems ever arise. The truth is that a book is no substitute for personal experience, and often nowadays the advice of grandparents is not readily available to young parents. Years ago many helpful tips could be got by a young mum listening to advice from her own mother. Such advice is often not available to today's young parents who are more likely to be living long distances from their relatives. This lack of family support is especially important for young and inexperienced parents, often living in large cities without friends or neighbours. One of the biggest problems is the growing number of mothers who have to bring up children, especially boys, on their own.

'Will it be difficult to change my child's behaviour?'

Probably. A child who is used to being cock of the roost is not going to take too kindly to parents trying to change the rules to his disadvantage. He is going to fight tooth and nail, and will not easily be convinced that his parents really mean business.

Things may get so hot and heavy that parents decide that changing his behaviour is just not worth the effort. Fine. It must be their own decision whether they carry on or give up – some behaviours are more important than others, some can be tolerated more easily than others. If at any time the stakes appear too high, then parents must be able to withdraw and concede defeat. Whether a child *must* go to bed at 10 o'clock or whether it is really not the end of the world if he stays up until midnight is a decision that cannot be made by a therapist. Similarly, only a parent can decide whether forcing a child to eat spinach is worth the effort involved.

Of course, not all decisions can be left to parents. A child who refuses to go to school will sooner or later come to the attention of the authorities and then the problem may be taken out of parental hands altogether.

With firmness and determination, mixed with concern and love, anything is possible. The keywords are *motivation* and *consistency*. Here are two real-life examples where they were missing.

The abetted arsonist

Nurse therapist: You say that Eric (who is seven) has lit three fires, one of which gutted your home and almost killed the whole family?

Mother: That's right. It scares the hell out of me just to think about it.

Nurse therapist: How did he get the matches?

Mother: From us. We're both smokers.

Nurse therapist: Have you given up smoking?

Father: Oh, no, we couldn't! It's a bad habit, we know, but neither of us could give up. (They laugh at the very suggestion.)

Nurse therapist: Then you've made sure that there are no matches in the house? I guess you're using a lighter and that you always carry it around on you and never leave it anywhere.

Mother: Ah, well, we tried that, and we both lost them. . . .

Nurse therapist: So you still use matches?

Father: Yes.

Nurse therapist to mother: Where are your matches now? (She produces them from her bag.)

Nurse therapist to father: And yours?

It turned out that father had left his matches at home on the mantlepiece.

A lack of motivation? This degree of short-sightedness in a serious and life-threatening situation is very unusual. A more common situation is when a son who is always stealing money has parents who refuse to lock away their cash because they 'don't want the house turned into a prison'. They want to feel that they can trust their son, although he may have shown them time and time again that they cannot. It is the parents' choice.

A teenage tippler

Trevor, a fourteen-year-old boy, had been picked up by the police after trying to break into a shop whilst drunk. His parents were well-off and there were always ample supplies of alcohol around the house. It turned out that Trevor had been drinking his parents' gin regularly for years and even suffered minor withdrawal symptoms when he could not get supplies. Father was aghast and resolved to lock up all the alcohol in the house and keep the key on his keyring. Mother also disapproved of her son pilfering the family booze but, unknown to father, would often share her gin and tonic with Trevor when father was not around. She also made no great attempts to prevent her son knowing where she kept her key to the drinks cabinet.

Lack of consistency? (And probably much more.)

Conclusion

It is to be hoped that the importance of motivation and consistency has been highlighted by these examples of potentially dangerous behaviours.

3

Ignore it!

A behaviour need not necessarily be changed – it may simply be ignored.

Tubby and teased

A loving mother would always wish she could somehow take the place of a child in order to show him that it *is* possible to ignore the taunts of others. In a similar way, therapists who are consulted about children's behaviour often wish they could take the place of the parents for a day or so in order to convince them that one of the most effective methods of combating unacceptable behaviour is to ignore it totally!

Sheila, an overweight thirteen-year-old with a brace on her teeth, is forever being teased by the other children at school. Her mother is reluctant to go and speak to the teachers in case it makes matters worse, so she decides to make use of her own experience of being teased when she was a teenager: 'If you can just ignore them, they'll soon get fed up. But remember – when they see you're not getting upset like you usually do, it'll encourage them to call you even worse names.'

Good, solid and sensible advice.

The process of extinction

In Chapter 1 reference was made to *pay-offs* or *reinforcers*. These are the rewards people get for behaving as they do; they also help to ensure that people will act in exactly the same way in the future. The reinforcer for the children to continue teasing Sheila is her obvious distress at being called names. Baiting

Sheila is a great spectator sport, and her predictable reaction guarantees that her classmates will have another go whenever they feel bored and in need of a little light entertainment. What her mother was trying to do was to get her daughter to practise *extinction*. This does not mean, though Sheila would dearly wish it, that the teasing children are suddenly zapped, destroyed or otherwise permanently removed. Instead, it refers to the possibility of extinction (stopping) of the teasing by withholding the reinforcement that keeps it going (Sheila's visible distress).

This may seem a very complicated explanation of a rather simple idea, but the principle of extinction can be used to get rid of many of the commoner behavioural problems displayed by children. The first and most important question that must be put to the parents is: Can you possibly ignore this bad behaviour? Because if you can, there is a good chance that it will soon stop.

The whinging princess

Let us see how extinction worked in Tracey's case. Tracey is six years old and the only child of loving parents. She is usually a warm, sweet and friendly child, the apple of her father's eye. He calls her his 'little princess', which, though it is not very original, does accurately reflect the way she has of twisting him around her little finger. Mother, who loves Tracey just as dearly, has only one major complaint – Tracey's habit of whinging whenever she does not get what she wants. If there is the slightest delay between Tracey's asking for something and getting it, she starts to whinge and whine, on and on and on, until in sheer exasperation mother stops whatever she is doing and gives her daughter what she demands. Father does not get the whinging because he always gives his daughter what she wants immediately.

In this situation it is easy to see why mother's pleas for Tracey to stop whinging fall on deaf ears. There is no reason on earth for Tracey to give up the most powerful method she has of getting her own way. Her whinging is constantly being paid-off or reinforced by mother giving her attention and then giving in to her wishes. It is simply *because* mother finds this behaviour so irritating that she acts quickly in order to stop it. Fine for Tracey's sense of control over grown-ups, but not so good for mother's self-esteem and mental health.

To outsiders the answer is obvious: simply ignore the little madam and she is bound to stop eventually – but be prepared for things to get worse before they get better. Mother's friends have been saying this for years; so has her own mother and even her mother-in-law. Father, on the other hand, whilst appearing outwardly sympathetic, thinks that his wife is apt to exaggerate the problem. Nevertheless, father is eager to play the role of dutiful husband and parent, and promises his wife total support in her efforts to gain some modicum of parent-power.

The approach: inaction stations!

The family came to an outpatient appointment and were seen by a nurse therapist and myself. After a long discussion of the problem in order to make sure we were not missing something important, we decided on a plan of campaign. Monday was fixed as D-day, and in the run-up period over the preceding weekend both parents were to take every opportunity to explain to Tracey that from now on 'whinging is out'. Tracey appeared to understand and there was great optimism of an early success. Monday morning went marvellously. Tracey attempted one whinge, was promptly reminded of the new house rules, and then went quietly away to make tea for her dollies.

The afternoon started badly. The first assault of whinging was soon after the meal when Tracey's mother refused to let her have a chocolate biscuit. Mother ignored her, and told Tracey how disappointed she was that she should have forgotten so soon all that they had been talking about. Tracey showed no remorse and continued to persist in her demands, whinging and groaning louder each time. The behaviour came as no surprise to mother since it was what she had been told to expect – the more Tracey whinged, the more mother became convinced that it was quite unseemly for a six-year-old child to get the better of an adult.

The attack gathered momentum all through the afternoon. Wave after wave of nerve-stretching Chinese torture pushed mother's patience to the limit...and beyond. Mother finally threw up her hands in despair and surrendered the biscuit barrel. Immediately after capitulating mother felt an over-whelming anger and frustration, directed both at her daughter and at herself. She snatched the biscuit back from out of the

child's hand and landed a generous smack on the little princess's rear end. Tracey, unused to such a reaction, retreated
into the Wendy house to cry with her dolls. Tracey's tears
pushed mother's guilt to unbearable heights. Overcome with
remorse she sought out her daughter and cuddled and kissed
away the pain of the smack.

When father came home and asked how things had gone,
Tracey relished recounting every detail, especially about how
much the smack had hurt. Father looked disbelievingly and
then disapprovingly at mother and commented that perhaps
the idea had not been such a good one after all.

Game, set and match to Tracey.

When ignoring the behaviour does not seem to work

From the comfort of our armchairs we can all think of lots of
reasons why Tracey won and mother lost. Although it is easy to
be wise after the event, nevertheless some valuable lessons can
be learnt.

Put bluntly, mother blew it because Tracey was still able to
get to her. The daughter played a better hand and won the
game. It is possible that mother might just have salvaged the
situation after the smacking (no moral judgements about the
smack – it happens to the most saintly of us!) if only she could
have coped with her guilt. It was the guilt that ensured that
Tracey got what she wanted, and more besides. Although no
blame attaches to Tracey for capitalizing on her advantage
when her father returned home – after all she is only six years
old – father can be severely censured for siding with his daughter against his wife.

This is a classic case of a mother, unsupported by her husband, who simply was not able to ignore her child's whinging
for long enough to bring about a change of behaviour.

Let us now consider temper tantrums, a common form of
bad behaviour in children, and one which is often amenable
to extinction therapy.

Temper tantrums

Every child has temper tantrums at some time or other – in fact
a normal three-year-old may have two or three a week. But that

is small comfort to the harassed mother whose son or daughter has two or three a day, week in, week out. There is no such thing as a 'typical' temper tantrum – which is precisely why I am going to describe one for you!

The child is usually under five years old and is just as likely to be a girl as a boy. (In children over five, temper tantrums usually merge into more extravagant and aggressive episodes of 'acting out' and these are much more serious.) Virtually anything can set off a temper tantrum.

'Shane versus scholarship'

Let us suppose that a three-year-old boy, Shane, has decided he wants to watch his favourite cartoon show at the very time when his mother's Open University programme on *Treasures of Renaissance Europe* is showing on the other channel. Let us further assume a degree of poverty in the family, i.e. that Shane does not have his own TV in the bedroom and that there is no video recorder in the house!

Shane bounds up to the TV and, quite oblivious to mother who is deep in concentration, switches channels. Bugs Bunny suddenly appears where once sat Lorenzo the Magnificent. Mother, used to her son's lack of social graces, flicks back to her programme, using the remote control. Shane reflexively presses the button on the set. Kartoon Kapers alternates with medieval Florence until Shane, realizing that it is time to play his ace, launches into his 'act', a temper tantrum that he knows from experience will end with him getting his own way.

Anatomy of a tantrum

He starts by giving out an ear-shattering scream, loud enough to be heard in the next street. This is accompanied by a violent shaking of the body (this bit he knows will scare mother most, though he is not sure why) and rapid colour changes of the face – first a florid red and then a frightening shade of blue as he holds his breath. He then throws himself on to the floor, crashing his fists repeatedly into the carpet. All this time the screaming gets louder and more continuous. It is these blood-curdling yells, his *pièce de résistance*, that usually bring instant surrender. Mother, her emotions a mixture of anger (verging on

infanticide) and concern that Shane may trigger an epileptic fit or apoplexy, weakly flicks over to the cartoons. She persuades herself that she will be able to get the gist of the programme from a student friend, or else she can get up at 6 a.m. on Sunday to catch the repeat.

A very powerful weapon

Shane admirably demonstrates the power of the temper tantrum and the speed with which it can produce the desired results. Parents capitulate for a number of reasons, but first and foremost because they decide that it is just not worth the aggravation and nervous tension of continued resistance. Fear of what the neighbours will think is also a potent cause of parental surrender, as is fear that the child may do himself permanent damage. The guilt that a parent would feel if any harm came to the child is an emotion that the youngster can use to great advantage. He is too young to understand what exactly it is that mother is afraid of; all he knows is that shaking his arms and legs and making his eyes bulge work wonders in getting his own way.

In Shane's case there was another potent source of maternal guilt – the guilt of self-indulgence. What right has she to deny her son the pleasure of TV cartoons? What on earth is she doing studying such irrelevant stuff? Perhaps father is right in thinking that the whole idea is stupid and that her job is to bring up his son and not dream about Florentine art treasures.

With so many things working in Shane's favour, is there any hope at all that mother can change his behaviour? A neighbour suggests that she should try to ignore him.

Can you ignore a temper tantrum?

The answer to this question usually depends on the child's age. It is often easy to ignore temper tantrums in younger children, but they can become much more difficult to ignore as the child grows older. The risk of a child bringing on a real epileptic fit in a temper tantrum is exceedingly low. I have never seen or heard of a case of this happening, though I admit there must be a possibility of a fit occurring in a child who has already been diagnosed as epileptic. It is the very natural parental anxieties about possible medical consequences that make temper tantrums such powerful and effective weapons with which a child can manipulate an adult.

Let us return to Shane and assume that mother has decided that in future she will not be brow-beaten into giving in to him whenever he wants something. She is determined that, come hell or high water, she will ignore his next outburst. Naturally she is just a little apprehensive about what might happen and she has to remind herself constantly that in all these years of temper tantrums Shane has never hurt himself badly. One bruised knee and one sore finger are the sum total of his injuries to date.

Mother goes to great lengths to tell Shane that from now on she is not going to take any notice of his tantrums. He does not believe a word of it – he has heard it all before. It is not long before Shane puts mother's resolution to a severe test. Over some trivial incident about taking his plate into the kitchen Shane decides to launch straight into a full-blown tantrum. He throws himself on to the sofa, shouting and kicking, pausing at intervals so as not to miss the familiar: 'OK! OK! I give in! Anything for a peaceful life! Poor Mrs Brown must think I'm killing you!' When the expected surrender does not come Shane is momentarily confused. He moves up a gear, screaming more loudly, thrashing about more theatrically – he even makes an attempt to kick the dog but Patch is too quick for him.

Nerves of steel

There is still no reaction at all from mother, who is pretending to be deeply engrossed, listening to a radio programme. She has worked out for herself that things will get worse before they get better, and sure enough, they do. Shane, quite confident that this is merely a temporary set-back, is determined to go all the way – shaking, thrashing, screaming, kicking. When he deliberately hits his hand on the table mother's resolve almost falters.

When even this performance fails to elicit any response, Shane uses a brand new strategy suggested to him by his friend Mark. He decides to go into overdrive and starts to bellow four-letter words at the top of his voice, calling his mother every obscene name he can think of. Although she is deeply shocked and angry at the swearing, mother has the presence of mind not to betray her emotions. She carries on listening to her programme as intently as if she were attending a lecture at a university, inwardly relieved that Shane's new weapon is verbal rather than physical. She is briefly uneasy about what Mrs Brown would make of this colourful vocabulary, but is determined that her neighbour's finer feelings should take second place to her own peace of mind and her son's long-overdue social education.

Eventually – and it feels like hours – Shane's performance starts to lose some of its momentum. After 10 minutes he takes a rest to recharge his batteries and take stock of the situation. Mother, waiting for just this opportunity, but appearing still to be fully absorbed in *Brain of Britain*, says: 'Here's a sweet, darling'. Shane throws the sweet across the room, toppling a glass off the dining table. He waits for a reaction but gets none, despite the fact that mother has frozen, fearful of what might happen next.

Seconds out: round two

After a pause Shane starts up again, but somehow his heart does not seem to be in it any longer. After another three or four minutes he stops again, this time taking an even longer break. Mother promptly smiles and says: 'Here's another sweet'. This time, although he does not eat the sweet, he does not throw it away either.

There is no need to go into any great detail about what happened subsequently. Predictably, Shane's tantrum gradually lost momentum, he took longer and longer rest periods, and began to realize that nothing he did would change his mother's mind about him having to take his plate out into the kitchen. He decided it would be much more sensible to give in this time and lay plans to fight another day. Besides which, he had quite a number of sweets now, and it was very difficult to scream and eat sweets at the same time.

After depositing the plate in the sink, Shane took himself off to his bedroom. When mother went to see how he was, she found him sulking and eating sweets. He looked away as soon as she came in. Determined not to gloat she went up to her son and gave him a big hug and kiss. She made no effort to apologize for anything that had happened – indeed, she took the opportunity to tell him kindly but firmly that the same thing would happen from now on every time he had a temper tantrum. She made a point of including father whenever she explained the new rules of the household. 'Daddy and I have decided. . . .'

Practical considerations about ignoring behaviours

It would be great to be able to report that Shane never had another temper tantrum, but it would not be true! Books about behaviour modification are full of page after page of successes with never a hint of failure. Before we find out why Shane's temper tantrums did not disappear, let us list the essential points to be considered when deciding to ignore temper tantrums.

1. It is important for experts to listen to parents, since they are the people who know the child best. If they are certain that their child will start to become destructive or aggressive then it is obviously going to be much more difficult to ignore the behaviour. It was an accident when the sweet broke the glass and mother was able to continue ignoring it. But if a child is the type who would deliberately go over to the glass and throw it against the wall then such behaviour is usually impossible to ignore. Some parents decide that they will remain alert to danger and intervene promptly if things start to get out of hand – mind you, as soon as one stops ignoring the behaviour, the child is getting the very attention he needs to continue the battle of wills.

2. Shane's mother thought that it would take hours and hours for him to calm down. She had even decided that the family would have to have a take-away because she probably would not have time to cook a meal. Most people overestimate the time a child will take to become quiet. Three or four hours is a common guess, and many parents become convinced that ignoring behaviour is not the answer simply because they do not have that much time to spare. In the experience of most therapists it is unusual for a child to continue the tantrum for more than half an hour or so. Many parents tend to disbelieve this but one can only

reiterate that tantrums lasting over 30 minutes without a break are *very* unusual. Of course, they can start up again after a break, but each subsequent tantrum will last a shorter and shorter time.

This is only logical. When a parent starts to ignore behaviour it is natural that a child will 'turn up the temperature'. But when it becomes obvious that there is no possibility of getting his own way, even the most determined child will eventually throw in the towel. Of course the child hopes that it will be the parent throwing in the towel – after all, winning is what counts.

Positive reinforcement

Another technique that Shane's mother made use of was *positive reinforcement*. This meant that as soon as he was quiet she gave him a sweet. Eventually he began to associate temper tantrums with uncomfortable and angry feelings, and quiet periods with rewards of sweets. Further consideration will be given to positive reinforcers in another chapter but research has shown that a combination of ignoring the bad behaviour and immediately rewarding the first sign of acceptable behaviour is more likely to succeed than ignoring on its own.

Shane's mother did brilliantly and deserved to succeed. Why then did she fail? The answer was a mixture of complacency and betrayal.

What went wrong?

Shane went away to lick his wounds and take stock. He was totally unused to not getting his own way and it was a severe blow to his ego. Of course, he still loved his mother, but was not very happy about this new stricter version. He would have another go at reasserting his authority the next day.

Mother was an intelligent woman and knew that the war would not be lost or won on the result of a single skirmish. She fully expected Shane to have another go at getting back to the 'good old days'. And sure enough he did. And mum won the next time as well. And the next time. And the next time.

Each time Shane was confronted by his new, highly motivated mother, each tantrum became shorter in intensity and duration than the previous one. After two weeks (during which, ordinarily, there would have been 30 or more tantrums) there were only five. In the two weeks after that there was only one. And in the two weeks after that there was none at all. The result of mother asserting her parental authority was that Shane became a much more loving and lovable boy.

Unfortunately in the second month things returned to being as bad as ever. Everyone had become complacent at the change brought about in Shane's behaviour and vigilance (i.e. consistency) had started to slip. This often happens, but usually there is such a new atmosphere of mutual collaboration in a family that a little more flexibility is both welcomed and appreciated. That is, the rules may be relaxed just a little, now and again, and no long-term disasters ensue. Of course, the only sure advice is to be totally inflexible when one discovers parent-power – the problem is that compromise is the stuff of life and the hope is that children will somehow view the occasional bending of the rules as an act of love and not an act of weakness.

Shane saw it as weakness. Things started to slide back at the time when mother was laid low by a particularly incapacitating monthly period which made her weak and dizzy and confined her to bed for three days. Mother recognized that she and father had become too complacent at their success and that Shane was one of the minority of children with whom inflexible attitudes to unacceptable behaviour have to continue for a great deal longer if permanent change is to take place. It is often a painful setback but it need not be a philosophy of despair – it simply means that until the child is much older, and hopefully more mature, he must remain on a very tight rein.

When granny does not toe the party line

Shane's mother was only just out of her sick bed when she had to go on the Open University summer residential school. This had been known months in advance and arrangements were made for Shane to go and stay with his granny in Wales. The Welsh half of the family had never approved of higher education for women and granny was especially scathing in her comments about her daughter-in-law's academic pretensions. Nevertheless a combination of circumstances – including father's trip abroad on business, the fact that mother's own parents were dead, and the fact that granny doted on Shane as he did on her – made the stay in Wales the logical choice. A fateful one as it turned out, especially at a time when Shane's behaviour was already deteriorating.

Many children show a different face to their grandparents than they do to their parents. It is quite usual for temper tantrums to be unknown when a child is with his grandparents. But this was not the case with Shane. His granny in Wales was subjected to the full force of his temper whenever he was thwarted or crossed or denied something he wanted. The old lady always gave in immediately. That was why Shane liked going there to stay. He would invariably return home laden down with expensive presents and bedecked in designer clothes. Mother had gone to great lengths to tell her mother-in-law that Shane's temper tantrums were a bad habit that they were trying hard to eradicate. She explained in minute detail the new regime. She could see that granny was not really listening, and dearly wished she could lodge Shane with someone else.

The inevitable happened and Shane returned more prone to temper tantrums than ever before. Granny had scuppered, either consciously or subconsciously, well-meaningly or maliciously, all efforts at behaviour modification.

Such an outcome is not unusual. The 'rubbishing' factor is most often father. Next comes granny (father's mother, usually), father's brothers and sisters, mother's brothers and sisters, friends, neighbours and so on. All the painstaking work done by one party is unpicked and reversed by another, either overtly or covertly.

The lessons to be learnt

There are two lessons to be learnt from Shane's story:

1. Parents must try to do all they can to get everyone on their side. They must persuade other people to cooperate for the benefit of the child.
2. If granny does not play according to the rules, then stop her playing at all.

In Shane's case, and assuming mum felt strongly enough about the matter, she would have been perfectly justified in stopping all contact between Shane and granny until granny gave a solemn undertaking to cooperate.

Those who baulk at this last piece of advice sometimes shout 'foul' because they maintain it is not granny's fault that Shane is the way he is. Maybe, but it might be seen as granny's duty to help try and civilize Shane before his behaviour patterns become carved in stone and impossible to alter. One child seen at the unit some years ago had just such a granny. The parents seemed resolved to start ignoring their daughter's behaviour up until the point when the therapist raised the question of grand-parents. It immediately became obvious that father relished the idea of telling his mother-in-law to stop meddling in their granddaughter's upbringing and leave the business of rules and discipline to the parents. It was just as obvious that his wife had not the slightest intention of allowing him to say anything of the sort to her mother. . . . Granny was not told and the child continued as out of control as ever.

When, and when not to, practise extinction

There are quite a number of obvious examples of behaviours where extinction is a logical way of approaching problems. Very young children whose aggressive instincts can be easily contained are definitely the best bet – whining and whinging toddlers are classical examples where this method can work wonders very quickly. The only drawbacks are the neighbours (who shall be considered in more detail in a later chapter) and grannies (by which is meant all types of well-meaning but unhelpful relatives).

It is usually easier to ignore verbal bad behaviour than physical bad behaviour. Consequently, children's bad language is a good candidate for extinction. (There are alternative ways of combating swearing which will be discussed later.)

Destructive urges are usually extremely difficult to ignore, though one example occurred when the parents were prepared to sit immobile and seemingly unconcerned whilst their nine-year-old son proceeded to destroy virtually everything in the house. For the record, that particular boy was cured of all further bad behaviour and was a 'different person' from then on, but it took more guts than most of us possess, so I feel very diffident about recommending it.

A last thought

At the start of an extinction programme consistency is essential. A child who sees that his parents are united and determined is much more likely to alter his behaviour sooner than a child who detects faltering motivation. Remember the analogy of the pen. *The message*: Once you have made up your mind, be determined to *stick to it* no matter what.

4

Granny's rule

It might be felt from what has been said in previous chapters that behaviour therapists hold a grudge against grandparents, and grannies especially. Therefore it is ironic that one of the most hallowed principles of behaviour modification is named after a granny. Simply stated, Granny's rule says: Eat your greens, then you can go out to play.

It is nothing more complicated than a tit-for-tat agreement whereby one person does something for another *provided* the other person does something in return. You eat your peas and cabbage *then* I will give you a reward (I will allow you out to play).

When cynics call it blatant bribery, most authors of books on behaviour modification look aghast and claim it is nothing of the sort since that would be quite unethical. All I say is, if it is not bribery, it comes pretty close.

Rewards and punishments

One of the fundamental aspects of using a tit-for-tat method of improving a child's behaviour is that a lot of thought is given to what you are going to use as a bribe – or rather, reward. There are some things that all children like, but they do not necessarily like them to the same degree. For example, if six-year-old Sarah likes a daily glass of cola, it does not follow that she is going to change her whole behaviour in order to get it. Failure to grasp this simple fact is the main reason why reward systems sometimes appear not to work.

Many parents say that their children are TV addicts and that they would do anything just to keep watching. It is not everyone's experience. Even though on a typical night a child might be glued to the TV set seemingly regardless of the programme, one finds that the 'price' a child might pay to continue watching a favourite programme like *Jim'll Fix it* or *The A Team* will be a lot more than he would be prepared to consider for other, less preferred programmes. Parents must also be aware of the marvels of our technological age: one father could not understand why his son seemed so oblivious to missing *The Dukes of Hazzard*, his *favourite* favourite programme – until he realized that his pal next door was videoing it for him.

If you do not know what a child likes best, ask him!

A lot of time needs to be spent working out a reward system for a child, since a little thought and imagination can pay great dividends. The most sensible way to start is to ask the child himself what he would most like as a reward for good behaviour.

Some parents think that the child will give deliberately wrong answers in order to foul things up, but on the very rare occasions when this happens, it is usually done in a very silly and obvious way which fools no one. More often children get angry and embarrassed when their bad behaviour is being discussed in detail by their parents and will react by saying nothing at all. A good tip is to keep things as informal as possible and to start by talking about the good things about the child before you get on to the bad. Some parents find it very difficult to think of anything good to say about a child, but every child does have good points and a little thought beforehand will prevent awkward silences when a child says that he is 'not always so bad'.

If, despite a softly-softly approach, a child is determined to be unhelpful, then obviously mother and father will have to compile the list of rewards on their own. One of the best ways of doing this is to ask parents to think through a typical day, jotting down the kinds of things that their child seems to enjoy and look forward to and also to make a list of the things the child does *not* enjoy. It is even better if lists are made up independently and then compared. In this way a greater variety of rewards is likely to be thought of.

Remember: rewards do not have to cost money. One need

not be buying expensive computer toys or organizing expensive trips to Alton Towers: sometimes it is materialism substituting for affection that had something to do with causing the child's behaviour in the first place! It is amazing the lengths that some children will go to for a kiss or cuddle or a word of praise from a previously uninterested parent – and kisses and cuddles cost nothing!

Two contrasting lists

Here are two lists made by parents, one which was done reluctantly, in a hurry and with almost no thought. The second list shows definite signs of imagination and flair.

List 1
Robert likes:
  Crisps
  Coke
  Chips, especially chip butties
  TV – anything

List 2
Patrick likes:
  Salt and vinegar crisps
  Bacon, egg and chips followed by tutti frutti icecream
  Going to bed late
  Getting up late at weekends
  Sandy, his dog
  A shandy at Sunday lunchtimes
  Grange Hill and *Dempsy and Makepeace*
  Gran in London, *not* Gran in Leeds
  Fishing, especially with dad
  Starting up dad's car
  Money, money, money
  . . .

The second list went on for more than a page and was proof of the trouble that these parents had taken in an effort to get to grips with their son's problem behaviour and how they might change it.

Punishments

Take away a reward and you have a punishment. Punishments for Patrick included going to bed early, having to get up early, having to have a lemonade on Sundays just like his younger sister, not being able to have Sandy sleep at the end of his bed, not being able to go fishing, forfeiting pocket money and so on and so on. A reward may also be the opportunity to get out of doing a chore, such as being let off having to clean the hamsters. People who feel uncomfortable about involving a pet in a behavioural programme will obviously not include items concerned with dogs and cats in their lists of rewards and punishments.

'Positive' punishments, i.e. those which are not just rewards in reverse, might include having to hoover and do the washing up, being forced to go to church whether they want to or not, or having to visit Great Aunt Elsie (who does not even have a TV).

Getting down to the nuts and bolts of an agreement

Motivation

It is taken for granted that there is high motivation in both parents, since examples have already been cited of how easily unenthusiastic fathers can virtually guarantee the failure of attempts to change a child's behaviour. It is necessary for fathers to have a large investment in seeing a change for the better, especially when it concerns behaviour that he never witnesses, such as disobedience to mother when he is at work.

Family conference

Sometimes a family conference called to discuss rewards and punishments is all that is required to produce a remarkable change in a child's behaviour. (This phenomenon is akin to the magical way a toothache disappears on the day of a dental appointment.) In such instances it is often the unusual sight of parents united in their shared concern that is enough to bring about the change. Sometimes it is the first occasion that a father has actually sat down for any length of time in order to talk to his children! If such a change in behaviour does happen, be sure to praise and reward the child constantly – it saves an enormous amount of work involved in a behavioural programme.

Lists of behaviours, rewards and punishments

If a family meeting fails, then father and mother should set aside time to make three lists each: a list of behaviours to be changed, a list of rewards, and a list of punishments. They then come together to compare notes and draw up a final master-list. It is sensible at the start to limit the list of behaviours to be changed to the three or four major ones – after all, if the first programme works well, the other bad behaviours may change spontaneously.

Prioritizing behaviours

Sometimes there is only one problem behaviour, but most often there are many, and they must be put in order of priority. This does not always mean that the most serious behaviour is put top of the list: it is sometimes easier to begin with a less serious behaviour, especially if the parents think that it is likely to come under control quicker. For instance, it may be thought that getting him to bed at a reasonable time will be easier to achieve than stopping him swearing at his mother, even though the swearing is the more worrying problem.

Honing definitions of bad behaviour

Having decided on the priority behaviour, it is necessary to be quite sure that each parent is agreed on the good behaviour which should take its place. This is not always as simple as it sounds. For instance, not all four-letter words are rude, and not all rude ones are rude to the same degree. Mother and father may have different ideas as to what is acceptable and what is not. There is really no alternative other than making a list of *all* banned words, even if some – those you didn't even know existed – have to be added later.

If the agreement is that a child should eat his vegetables,

does this mean *all* vegetables, or just carrots and peas? If he must be in by 7 o'clock, is this 7 o'clock on the dot or 7 o'clock plus a margin of five minutes? If a child has to help with the housework, what exactly does that mean? If it is hoovering, how often, which rooms, and does it mean behind the sofa? All these details may seem trivial, but they are a severe test of motivation. Poor motivation is accurately reflected in badly thought out behavioural programmes which often end up making matters much worse than they were before.

Pause: If all this seems like too much trouble, perhaps you should be discussing with the parents whether they can, after all, put up with their child's behaviour just as it is and not have to spend valuable time and energy trying to change it. Just a reminder that there is always a choice!

A case of hyperactivity

By way of example, I will use the case of Roger, a six-year-old boy who never seemed to be still for more than a few seconds. He had been diagnosed as 'hyperactive', like his cousin. Special diets had been tried in the past and had had no effect.

Choosing a target behaviour

Of all the various behaviours indulged in by children, there will be some that parents will disapprove of and want to change and others, which are good and make you happy, that you will want to encourage. It is very important not to lose sight of the good things about a child's behaviour. If he is kind to animals or helpful to elderly neighbours, this must be mentioned and praised again and again. An endless catalogue of bad behaviours will only anger a child or make him feel that his problems are so great that he could never possibly change, even if he wanted to.

It is also important to increase the chances of success by focusing on a particular behaviour and concentrating all efforts on changing just that one behaviour. If that works you can then move on to others at a later time. As has been said, choosing a target behaviour is not always easy because different people have different views about the same behaviour.

To describe a child's behaviour as 'awful' or 'exasperating' is not very helpful. The particular awful or exasperating aspects of the behaviour have to be gone into in considerable detail in order to identify its essence.

'He's hyperactive' or 'He's overactive' are descriptions that many parents give to their children, but these are too broad to be useful in behaviour modification. What exactly is meant by 'hyperactive'? Here are some of the questions that a nurse therapist might ask in order to help the parents target a behaviour in a child who is thought to be hyperactive:

1. Does it mean that he is more active than his friends or classmates, or his brothers and sisters when they were his age?
2. Does it mean that he *never* rests, that he is *always* on the go from the time he gets up until the time he goes to bed?
3. Will he sit still long enough to have a meal or watch a favourite television programme?
4. What time does he wake in the morning and what time does he go to bed at night? Is it difficult to get him to go to bed at night? When he does go off to sleep, does he sleep all through the night? When he wakes in the morning, does he immediately get out of bed?
5. Does he stop being overactive if you tell him to? Will he listen to what you ask him to do?
6. Is he destructive with his toys? Does he break other children's toys?
7. Is he aggressive to other children or to adults?
8. Does he have temper tantrums if he is stopped from doing what he wants to do?
9. Is his behaviour worse in certain situations? For example, is he even more active when visiting other people's homes or is he always very good except in his own home? Is his behaviour just as bad at school and, if so, have the teachers complained?

All these questions will hopefully assist a therapist in helping parents to concentrate their efforts on a small aspect of the behaviour which is considered to have the best chance of being altered for the better. Most truly overactive children have great difficulty in staying still long enough to eat a meal with the rest of the family, and consequently adults get very fraught and short-tempered at mealtimes. Perhaps, then, it would be best to start with the child's behaviour at mealtimes. But even this is too general, too broad, and will need to be broken down into constituent parts:

1. Does he come for his meals when called? If not, how many times does he have to be called? Is it easier to get him to come on time to some meals rather than others, on some days rather than others?
2. When he does come, will he eat all his meal at a great pace or does he mess around so much that very little food is eaten? Does he interfere with other people eating their meals? Does he throw food around? Is he always getting out of his chair and having to be called back? Does he throw knives and forks on to the floor? Does he spit food out of his mouth? Does he give most of his food to the dog?
3. Does he stay at the table until everyone has finished? Does he leave the table and then have to be brought back for dessert? Is he allowed to eat his dessert away from the table?
4. Is he asked to help clear away the plates and cutlery? How many times does he have to be asked? Who does the asking? Is one parent more likely than the other to get him to do his jobs?

Roger's behaviour at mealtimes

It will be apparent that the greatest chance of successful behavioural modification comes from choosing a particular behaviour, analysing it in great detail and then writing down precisely the ways in which you want that behaviour to change. Let us stick to the overactive child, and assume that the parents have agreed to tackle Roger's table manners first. Let us further assume that Roger finds it very difficult to sit still and concentrate on the family discussion of his problems, and that during the short time he was present he only made silly suggestions about wanting icecream for breakfast, lunch, and dinner. The rest of the planning conference had to go on without him. His older sister Tanya, aged ten, was very eager to join in, and although it was thought that Roger's table manners had a large effect on her life – not least of which was the 'fallout' from arguments between mum and Roger — it was felt that the chances of Roger eventually joining in would be much less if he thought his sister was responsible for drawing up some of the rules.

The desired behaviour defined

It took about an hour to discuss and finally write down the essentials of the behaviour, how it should be changed and then put it into language that a six-year-old could understand. Here is the final result:

> Mum and dad love Roger very much and think that he is very kind, but they are not pleased with the way he behaves at the table when he is eating his meals.
>
> From now on Roger will come to the table for meals as soon as he is called by mum or dad. He will sit down quietly and eat his food and he will not spit food out of his mouth or throw food on the floor or give food to Lassie. When he has finished the main meal he will sit quietly and wait for afters. When he has finished afters he will take his plate and his knife, fork and spoon to the sink in the kitchen. He can then carry on playing.

There are bound to be things that should have been included but were forgotten. It will have to be decided if they are important enough to include at a later time or whether it would be too complicated to include them. For instance, father suggested that Roger might be asked to wash his hands before eating, but it was decided that this was not essential and would shift attention away from more important issues.

Here is the flow chart so far:

General list of behaviours to be changed
↓
Arrangement of the list in order of priority
↓
Accurate description of the target behaviour
↓
Accurate description of the behaviour you would like to take its place

How often is always?

The next chore (because most parents see it as an irrelevance) is to decide just how often the target behaviour happens. It is just plain silly to say 'always' or '99.999% of the time'. Unless it is accurately recorded how often a problem behaviour occurs, how will anyone be able to spot the beginning of an improvement – unless, of course, the improvement is sudden and total? Just because a behaviour is not cured immediately and just because it still appears to be going strong a week later, it does not mean that there has been no improvement. The target behaviour may have dropped from occurring ten times a day to seven. This might not seem a lot but it *is* a change in the right direction. Unless the frequencies of the target behaviour were being accurately charted, such a small but important change may have been missed and the whole programme abandoned too early as worthless.

Keeping a diary

In our example of Roger and his table manners there appears to be very little problem in charting frequencies, but it would still be worthwhile jotting down in a diary each meal that was made miserable by his behaviour. Everyone has a tendency to be selective in their memory. People only remember drunk Australians, loud-mouthed Americans or tight-fisted Scotsmen. Similarly, harassed parents forget the odd occasion when their child behaved well simply because he behaved so badly so many more times.

Accurate baseline records are even more important in behaviours that do not occur in such an obvious setting as Roger and mealtimes. Just how often does Sally not do as she is told? How often does John call his father 'stupid'? How often does Tim come into his parents' bed? If the behaviour is very common some days and not so common on others, then recordings may be needed over a couple of weeks to see if a pattern emerges. It is surely worth it if it increases your chances of ultimately being successful in lessening the particular behaviour.

Do not trust your memory. Write it down and do not be

embarrassed about keeping a diary. Some people feel uncomfortable about writing down a child's bad behaviour and think that somehow it is not what a good parent should do. If this worries you, write down the good behaviours as well. Diaries are best kept by each parent. If only mum keeps the diary and dad thinks it beneath him, or is always forgetting or insists that he can remember it without writing it down, then I would suspect that someone was lacking total commitment.

It is also very instructive to record the circumstances leading up to a particular behaviour. For instance, a child may be much more likely to defy a parent if one of his friends is around and he wants to show off. Or a child may only have a temper tantrum when mum is feeding the baby. Or getting up in the mornings may only be a problem on school days. The more details that can be recorded about what leads up to an episode of bad behaviour, the more you are likely to find out if that behaviour has any hidden significance.

Applying granny's rule

The next step – having identified the target behaviour, recorded how often that behaviour occurs and decided what behaviour to put in its place – is to apply granny's rule. Assuming that normal children act the way they do because it suits them, it is obvious that they are not going to change their ways unless they can be persuaded that there is something in it for them. Parents have to make a behaviour change worthwhile for the child. This is where the list of rewards and punishments comes in.

But remember: rewards need not always be things; they can also be acts, like praising, smiling, hugging, playing and so on.

Back to Roger. As he is six he is probably able to understand that rewards for good behaviour at the table will not be given immediately, but that he will have to wait until the end of the meal. We shall see later that whilst older children are often able to wait considerable periods before they get rewarded, younger children often have to be given their rewards immediately.

Listing rewards for Roger's good behaviour

Here is what Roger's parents decided in discussion with a nurse therapist. Each time he behaved himself at the meal table he would be given a chocolate bar, which he loved and could never get enough of, and a token. This token, which looked something like Monopoly money, was made by mum out of red cardboard and had written on it *one token* in large fancy writing. Every night the number of tokens won by Roger was totted up and the following rules applied:

Four tokens   = able to phone grandad at 7 o'clock
(the maximum number)   each day to say goodnight

Three tokens = allowed to have his friend Paul in to play from
             4 to 5 o'clock

Two tokens = allowed to have Paul in to play from 4 to 4.30

One token = no extra rewards

A great deal of fuss must be made of Roger if he manages to win tokens and an air of sadness rather than criticism must be conveyed if he wins no tokens. The kiss of death for any 'token economy' as it is called, is for a parent to say in a half-hearted fashion: 'That's good, now go and collect your token from the drawer in the sitting room'. The winning of a token must be an important event and it is impossible to be too enthusiastic about it. The more pomp and razzmatazz the better. For three or four tokens parents must be 'over the moon', and Dad, if he is out working, must return home ready to praise Roger up to the sky. A bored and tired father who pats Roger's head and says, 'Fine, keep it up' is ensuring that Roger will do anything but.

It goes without saying that Roger does not have Paul in to play if he does not win two tokens or more and will not, under any circumstances, be allowed to ring grandad unless he wins all four tokens. (Grandad must be thanked profusely for his cooperation in changing Roger's behaviour.)

It is a good idea to make tokens of different denominations out of different coloured paper. In this way, say, four single tokens can be exchanged for a bigger and more elaborate *four tokens* note at the end of the first day (hopefully). To keep up the momentum and interest, tokens should be totted up at the

end of a week and can be traded in for even better prizes. For example:

21–28 tokens = visit to the Planetarium with MacDonald's and chips on the way home

14–20 tokens = going swimming with dad at the local pool and being allowed to dive off the bottom board

7–13 tokens = a children's video of Roger's choice

0–6 tokens = no extra prizes

It can be seen that Roger has to behave well at more than one meal a day in order to get either a daily or weekly prize. If a child is too young to appreciate this fact immediately it must be explained to him again and again in language that he can understand.

There are a number of problems inherent in applying Granny's rule which will be discussed in Chapter 5.

5
More about token economies and star charts

Behavioural modification programmes benefit by being well thought out in order to predict as many snags as possible before they happen. The least plausible of Roger's excuses for continued bad behaviour must be that he did not know when the new regime was starting, or that he did not understand the new rules. It is worth having a 'countdown to D-day' so that on each day of the week before the programme is scheduled to begin, mum and dad can take every opportunity to remind Roger exactly what is planned, what the new behaviour is to be and all about the rewards and punishments that have been agreed. He should be kept up to date on all the refinements as they happen, even if he does not seem in the least bit interested. Most children will listen attentively, even though they pretend not to – if only to plan an effective counterattack!

The first reaction of many children is: 'They'll never keep it up'. This will often be based on half-hearted attempts that parents have tried in the past. History, the child thinks, is on his side. Nonetheless children sometimes become intrigued when the rules of the programme are written down and then signed by all parties with great pomp and ceremony. Because Roger would not give in to read the contract his parents drew up, it had to be left unsigned. We will return to consider how to draw up contracts a little later when we discuss Wendy.

Most parents begin a behavioural programme on Monday because that seems the logical day to start. Unfortunately, if all goes well, and Roger is on course for a trip to the Planetarium, the requisite number of tokens may not be earned before Saturday morning, and that could be too late to arrange or cancel an outing to London. Roger's patience and enthusiasm may fade dramatically if he is suddenly expected to wait until the next weekend for his reward. Therefore, a programme that runs from Saturday morning to the following Friday night has many advantages, not least of which is that everyone knows what the plans are for the weekend! As interest in the new programme begins to flag in the middle of the first week, a youngster's enthusiasm might be re-kindled by telling him how close he is to a possible major prize.

Star charts

Next the nurse therapist discussed the use of star charts. It is not unusual for parents to throw their hands up in horror and high-tail it for the door at the very mention of star charts. They groan: 'But we've tried them and they didn't work! He soon lost interest and didn't care whether he got his stars or not'. The truth is usually that the star charts *did* work initially, but it was the *parents* who lost interest and not the child. Quite simply, the parents became bored with having to appear enthusiastic every time a star was won. Little wonder that the child soon became disillusioned.

On the Friday before the programme was to start, Roger's father, an architect by trade, used all his skills to design an impressive-looking star chart according to intructions given by the therapist. He divided the chart into the days of the week with a space for each mealtime. He asked Roger to join in, but he was told to 'Piss off!' Dad made a mental note to have swearing high on the list of priorities for the future. Figure 5.1 shows what the chart ended up looking like.

The idea had been to discuss with Roger how to mark on the chart those meals when his behaviour had been good. However, Roger was still defiant and pretended not to know what his father was talking about. It had been hoped that Roger, who was an excellent artist, would crayon in trains or cars or fish (since he loves fishing) instead of stars. Reluctantly the parents decided they would have to use the sticky-backed stars they had bought from the newsagent.

Let us assume that out of the 28 meals (four each day) in the week before the programme started, Roger had managed to be badly behaved at 27 of them, and that the only clue that could

Roger's Star Chart

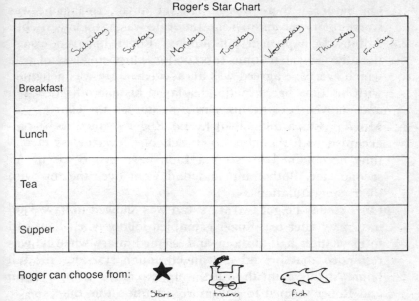

	Saturday	Sunday	Monday	Tuesday	Wednesday	Thursday	Friday
Breakfast							
Lunch							
Tea							
Supper							

Roger can choose from: Stars — trains — fish

Fig 5.1 Roger's star chart

be got for his good behaviour on that single occasion was that at the time he was not feeling very well. Having thus recorded the number of fraught mealtimes in an average week, let us have a close look at what happened in the first week of *Operation mealtime*.

	Sat	Sun	Mon	Tue	Wed	Thu	Fri
Breakfast				*			
Lunch						*	*
Tea		*	*	*	*	*	*
Supper					*		

Analysing the record

Interesting insights may be obtained from studying the chart. The nurse therapist helped the parents to analyse the record, and these are the points they noticed:

1. On Saturday there was no change at all. In fact he was worse than ever and parental morale was at its lowest ebb.

2. A miracle happened on Sunday. Roger behaved exceptionally well at teatime (except for a tipped glass of cola which everyone agreed was an accident). He was delighted with his Lion bar, proudly displayed his magnificent token and enjoyed sticking his very first star on the chart.

3. Monday was a difficult day, and Roger seemed to be preoccupied with thoughts about school. Nevertheless at teatime he obtained his second Lion bar, second token and second star. Both mum and dad went over the top with their congratulations.

4. On Tuesday he got two stars and was allowed to have Paul in to play after tea. Roger grumbled loudly when Paul had to leave after half an hour and seemed angry when he was reminded that he did not have enough stars for the full ·hour. At this point the rules were explained all over again and Roger seemed to pay more attention this time.

5. A different pattern emerged on Wednesday and the first real snag. Although two stars were won, Paul was not allowed in to play since by 5 o'clock only one star had been obtained. Both parents felt guilty about this and blamed themselves for not having foreseen this eventuality. It seemed an insurmountable problem and they feared that Roger felt let down. They also sensed that he was losing interest in Lion bars.

   It was also clear on Wednesday night, with six stars won, that the Planetarium was out of reach and that swimming with dad could only be got by earning all eight remaining stars. After discussion between the parents it was decided not to tell Roger of the inevitable shortfall in stars, and to drop all references to the Planetarium. They would also play down swimming, and concentrate on the video he could choose. But another problem arose here: Roger only had to get one more star for the video. Did he realize that he only had to behave well just once in the next eight mealtimes in order to get a video? They decided not to tell him.

6. Thursday was another good day – two more stars. The tally was now eight and the video was in the bag, but there was no possibility of swimming, and although Roger had

obviously worked this out for himself, he was going around the house talking about going to the pool. It was here that inconsistency crept in – father would not tell Roger that swimming was definitely off, whereas mother was honest and direct.

7. Friday was a day of mixed fortunes. Roger won two stars, making ten his week's tally. He had no need to win four stars in order to ring grandad since grandad came for lunch and took Roger back to school in the afternoon. A disaster was averted because, although Paul was ill in bed and so the two-star prize was impossible, grandad stayed on late and took his grandson for a walk by the lake instead.

8. Saturday came and Roger was deliberately harping on about swimming with dad, trying to weaken parental unity. He failed. Nevertheless, to show their appreciation of such a magnificent effort they went to town on the Saturday afternoon and had Danish pastries, Roger's favourite. They then came back and everyone watched and enjoyed Superman II, the video Roger himself won and chose.

Not a bad week's work for all concerned!

Good omens

It is important to recognize what contributed to the overall successful outcome:

1. A high degree of motivation and a large measure of consistency (except towards the end of the week).
2. Persistence despite an unpromising start.
3. The ability to improvise and substitute at the last minute, especially when Paul fell ill.
4. The large amount of interest and encouragement shown by mum and dad, and by grandad at the end of the week.

Consistency versus flexibility

The second and third weeks showed a continued though gradual improvement, each time Roger having enough tokens to cash in for a trip to the swimming pool. The fourth week started badly and both parents sensed that the rewards were going to have to be changed if Roger's interest was not to evaporate. This became especially urgent when Roger quarrelled with Paul and the swimming pool closed because the chlorination machine broke down! In the nick of time other rewards were substituted and the programme continued. After eight weeks Roger's behaviour at the table was exemplary.

As so often happens when a programme is successful, it was also noticed that Roger's general behaviour was showing marked signs of improvement. He was becoming less defiant, less argumentative and less aggressive. All this seemed to be helped by mum and dad going out of their way to praise him whenever his behaviour was good. Slowly dad even came to trust him with his special carpentry tools, and a deep bond began to develop between father and son.

So what might have gone wrong?

Almost anything, depending on the child, the parents and a million and one other things. It has been said before but can bear repetition many times: motivation and consistency are the greatest assets in making a behaviour modification programme successful. Nevertheless, since some common problems keep coming up time and time again, it is worth focusing attention on them.

Jealous brothers and sisters

This can be a very serious problem unless the parents recognize that well behaved siblings may feel genuinely aggrieved to see a bullying or foul-mouthed brother actually being given prizes and presents for being good – something that they have been doing for years for nothing. Older sibs do not *necessarily* understand any better than younger ones, so it is especially important to be sensitive to their feelings.

The answer is to reward the sib as well. Obviously it looks better if they actually have to do something for the reward. Many are asked to help with the washing up or run errands or tidy their rooms or make coffee for mother or do their homework on time or be generally helpful. Younger sibs can have a star chart of their own which can hang in a prominent place in the kitchen, in their bedroom etc.

Even when brothers or sisters are given a star chart of their own, it is still an easy thing for parents to give too much attention to the 'naughty' child at the expense of the 'good' one. The major weekly rewards also affect sibs, and it is understandable that they should feel upset if a trip to the Planetarium is cancelled just because a brother or sister has not behaved well enough. Solutions to this problem will vary: some sibs will be old enough to be reasoned with, others will be too young to appreciate fully what is going on, whilst yet others may be taken to the Planetarium anyway or else rewarded in some other appropriate way.

'It's a good idea but it can't start yet'

This is another common reason for failure – that there is never a good time to start. It is logical that it is probably a bad time to begin a behaviour modification programme on the day a child is to start a new school, or when he is due to go into hospital to have his tonsils out, or Christmas Day or the day of his sister's wedding. But there must be a limit to these restrictions or else nothing will ever get done. The most common reason for failing to start on time is probably that it is too near the beginning of term, too near the end of term or too near half-term. Other common ones are illnesses such as flu or sore throat (it is staggering how often these develop the very day a behavioural programme is to start!). Dad being on nights, sister doing O-levels and heavy snow have been other excuses.

A favourite is: 'He promised he would change so we postponed the programme'. In all cases of delayed start, the opportunity should be taken by the therapist to go over the main behaviour problem again and ask the parents if they are sure they cannot just put up with it and save themselves the bother of trying to change it.

Problems with the rewards

Paul's illness, and the fact that he and Roger quarrelled, could have sounded the death-knell to the success of the programme.

It is not easy to foresee all the possible problems that might arise but it is always helpful to have 'something for a rainy day', literally! Any reward that depends on fine weather is at potential risk, especially in this country, so it is important to have indoor alternatives for all outdoor rewards.

Of course, everything has the potential for going wrong, and it would be impossible and time-wasting to cover all contingencies. Nevertheless it would be wise to make sure you have a good stock of Lion bars or enough cola to last a weekend if these are the selected rewards.

The problem of a child who is old enough and bright enough to work out on Wednesday that he has no hope of gaining enough tokens by Saturday to win the top prize has no easy solution. To bend the rules can be seen as weakness and may be interpreted as impending victory by a child. On the other hand, to be too inflexible might persuade a child that it really is not worth going on. Some parents find that the answer is to improve the quality of the more immediate rewards, i.e. in Roger's case, to give 20p *and* a Lion bar. It is impossible to be dogmatic about this but, on the whole, it is better to err on the side of inflexibility (i.e. consistency) rather than make too many concessions too soon.

Wendy and the nightly battle of the bed

Wendy is the nine-year-old daughter of a single mother. She is an enormous help to mother in looking after her baby brother Simon, aged eight months. Unfortunately Wendy had become so much of a 'parental' child that she began to act more and more like someone twice her age. At first this precociousness was amusing, but recently her whole attitude to her mother had become unseemly for one so young. The major form of rebellion was the problem mother had in fixing a bedtime for Wendy. Wendy would insist on staying up until mother herself went to bed, and this would make her so tired the next morning that it was very difficult to get her up for school. Recently mum had got a boyfriend and Wendy's habit of staying downstairs was becoming particularly irksome.

The basis of an agreement

Eventually mother and Wendy agreed on a reasonable bedtime of 8.30 and mother started a system of immediate and delayed rewards. If Wendy went was in bed by 8.30 *and no later*, she would be allowed to read her magazines and comics until 9.30. If she kept to the new schedule for a week mother would allow her to go into town on Saturday with her friend Helen. She would also be allowed to wear a little lipstick and paint her nails. If she was not in bed by 8.30 for all seven consecutive nights then the trip to town and the agreements about make-up would be cancelled.

Some may baulk at the idea of trying to curb a nine-year-old's precocity by rewarding her with those very things that would make her look older than her years. Fair enough – but it was an agreement between a mother and daughter that worked very well, after an initial hiccup.

What mother had forgotten was that although Wendy was in her bed by 8.30 she felt that she was able to come out of her

T028468

room to go to the loo as often as she liked. That sounds very reasonable except that Wendy's bladder proved so weak that she was in and out of bed four or five times a night, and each time she would pop her head over the bannister to ask mother something or other. Because the new rules had not been spelt out in great detail, Wendy was tempted to flout the arrangement and then claim: 'I can't help it if I have to go to the loo!'

Re-negotiation and greater clarity in the form of a contract

The agreement was re-negotiated and set down in the form of a contract, so that there was very little chance of any further misunderstanding:

> This is an agreement worked out between Wendy and mum and witnessed by Peter Thomas on the 14th May 1986. Without having to be asked, Wendy agrees to be undressed and in her bed by 8.30 on Sunday, Monday, Tuesday, Wednesday, and Thursday nights. She is allowed to read until 9.30 but is not allowed to listen to her radio or play her records or tapes. At 9.30, without being told, she will turn off her light, whether she feels sleepy or not. She is not allowed to come downstairs or call out when Peter leaves. She will only be allowed to go to the loo once in the night, and she is then *not* to call down to mother or disturb the baby.
>
> On Friday and Saturday nights Wendy will be in bed by 10.00 but can read quietly until 10.30. She is not to play her radio or tapes and will go to the loo only once.
>
> In return for going to bed at the times stated every night mother promises to allow Wendy to go into town with Helen on the bus on Saturday afternoon. Wendy must be back home by 4.30. Wendy is allowed to wear lipstick – but only a shade that mother approves of – which will be put on by mother. Wendy is also allowed to have her nails varnished on Saturdays in a colour that mother approves of.
>
> If Wendy is not in bed by the times agreed she will not be allowed into town, will not be allowed to wear lipstick and will not be allowed to wear nail varnish.
>
> Signed: Mrs Jane Simmons
>
>   Wendy Simmons
>
> Witnessed by Peter Thomas.

Conclusion

Happily all went well and the behavioural programme was an instant and long-lasting success. But what, you may ask, would have happened if Wendy had defied her mother, since no punishments or penalties were mentioned in the contract. The whole question of punishments will now have to be discussed in the next chapter, with reference to Arthur.

6
Punishments

Arthur's tale

Arthur's father described him as a demon. His mother could never get him to do anything and his teacher said he was the rudest and most uncooperative seven-year-old she had ever come across in 30 years of teaching.

Arthur's parents came to the unit to have him 'put away' in care because they said they just could not cope, and because the arguments the boy was causing were going to wreck their marriage. The truth was that both of them loved him dearly and neither wanted to put him into care. In reality they had come in a desperate attempt to find an instantaneous solution, knowing full well that there was not one. At the very mention of star charts they were half way out of the door – if that was all the so-called experts had to offer, they may as well go and phone social services straight away!

Slowly they were reassured and parents and therapists got down to studying the problem in minute detail. Arthur sat on the opposite side of the room with his back to them, but listening attentively to every word. From bitter experience the parents knew a lot about behaviour modification and so Alison, the senior nurse therapist on the unit, went straight into drawing up lists of priorities, rewards and punishments.

There was no disagreement about the behaviour that irked the parents most. That was Arthur's habit of never doing what he was told. As you can imagine, the word 'never' is too broad to be very useful in planning behaviour modification, so the parents were sent away to keep a diary for a week and then come back and report. It turned out that Arthur defied his parents roughly 30 times a day, more at the weekends. He would either ignore his parents altogether or answer them

defiantly, often with foul language. According to his father, Arthur was immune to physical punishments and Dad had given up smacking his son a long time ago for fear that in his rage he would damage the boy permanently.

Visualizing the problem

A graph was plotted of Arthur's defiance and it looked something like this:

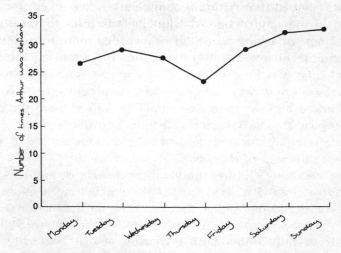

Fig 6.1 Graph of Arthur's behaviour

Apart from a slight rise at weekends, probably explained by the fact that he was around the house more, there seemed to be no pattern. It did not appear to matter who asked him or what he was asked to do. Thus the new behaviour was to be simply that Arthur would in future respond when he was asked to do something. If he ignored the first request he was to be warned that he would only be asked one more time, and told that if he refused to comply on being asked a second time he would not get any rewards, stars or tokens.

Preparing the star chart

A star chart and token economy was devised, each day being divided into morning (from the time he got up until 8.30 when he left for school), afternoon (from mid-day until 5 o'clock) and evening (from 5 o'clock until he went to bed – which could be virtually any time!). Although Saturdays are usually the best day to start (as in Roger's case), it was decided that Arthur's programme would start on a Monday. This was because since most of the morning and afternoon would be spent at school there was a better chance that he could pick up the morning and afternoon stars without too much trouble and therefore have a headstart by the time he came home to face the long evening period.

So much for the theory!

It was agreed that Arthur would be given five tokens for each period in the day: if he did what he was told at the first or second time of asking he would be awarded more tokens, up to a maximum of five in any one period. If he refused after the second time of asking he would lose tokens, one by one. The parents went to great pains to explain the programme to Arthur and showed him the things he would get (all of them things he was known to like) if his behaviour improved. Some really exciting things had been planned if he managed to get enough tokens at the end of the week.

Because young children find it difficult to wait any length of time for a reward it was decided that each time a token was given, i.e. each time Arthur did something at the first or second time of asking, he was also to be given a small sweet like a Smartie or Jelly Baby, both favourites of his. Naturally each token also represented a star, so he was to stick five stars on a chart for each period of the day, and a great fuss would be made of him whenever he won extra tokens and stars.

By 8.30 on Monday morning Arthur had lost all the five stars that he had been given to start with. By 6 o'clock in the evening his score was still zero and there it remained until he was finally bundled off to bed at 10.15! Each time mother or father (who was unemployed and at home all day) gave the warning, Arthur would shout and scream and kick, demanding Smarties. By the end of the second day, with Arthur's score still zero, mother's shins covered in bruises and with father claiming 'I'll swing for the little bugger!' they returned to see Alison to tell her where she could put her star chart.

Where did they go wrong?

Nowhere. It is a sad fact that despite all efforts some children simply refuse to change. Whether Arthur was one such child it was a little too early to tell.

What is to be done when a child seems hellbent on continued defiance, when he does not give a damn for any earned rewards, and when he launches dangerous attacks on anyone who tries to thwart or discipline him? The answer, short of care, is the judicious use of punishments.

Types of punishment

There are basically three ways of punishing a child:

1. Loss of tokens and stars.
2. Loss of other privileges.
3. Time out.

Arthur was quite immune to the first option.

The second option, loss of privileges, was tried next. These, too, had been decided upon beforehand and an effort had been made to discuss them with Arthur and include them in the contract (which, needless to say, he neither read nor signed). The actual punishments can only be chosen with the individual child in mind since what is a punishment for one child may be no punishment at all for another. The second golden rule in deciding upon which privileges are to be lost is never to threaten what you have no intention of carrying out. It is the failure to observe this rule that leads parents to utter elaborate threats about being banned from going out of the house for five years! These theatricals are definitely counterproductive.

In Arthur's case loss of privileges included not being able to watch TV, confiscation of toys and cancellation of his birthday party. One must guard against being judgemental about the punishments other parents choose for their own children. You should always ask yourself what *you* would instigate if your own child were to show such extremes of behaviour. Unfortunately, in Arthur's case, it appeared that TV was not as important to him as his parents had thought; he coped well without his favourite toys, and he appeared to take the cancellation of his party in his stride.

His parents began to talk again about care – unless time out could change him. Time out is a useful strategy, the intricacies of which will be explained in Chapter 7.

7
Time out

Time out has had a bad press. Recently an incredulous radio interviewer asked a visiting American psychologist if he was seriously advocating shutting a small child in the loo for misbehaving. The tone of the question suggested that this was a heinous crime never to be contemplated, let alone perpetrated against any child by civilized parents. In fact time out, or TO as it is commonly known, is one of the most effective ways of changing a child's behaviour, and is something that should be applied early in a behavioural programme.

Consider Arthur. Here we have a seven-year-old who was being defiant, shouting and screaming, kicking out at his mother and father. Mother decides to employ TO. She clasps him around his middle and deposits him gently but firmly in the downstairs loo. She tells him that he will remain in the loo for three minutes but that the time does not start until he is quiet.

Question: Assuming that all this had previously been explained to him and had not come as a bolt out of the blue, how long is it estimated that a child will have to stay in the loo before he calms down and is allowed out?

Answers will vary according to the intelligence and stubbornness of the child, but it is quite unusual for TO to last for more than about 30–40 minutes.

Assume for the moment that it lasts 30 minutes. Assume further that as soon as Arthur is released he immediately launches into another show of defiance even worse than the first. He is put back into the loo.

Question: How long is he likely to be in TO on this second occasion? Remember that the same rules apply – the three-minute period only starts when he becomes quiet.

One does not have to be a genius to predict that the TO will be a lot shorter than before. Probably no more than 10–15 minutes, if that long. The child will quickly learn that being in the loo is not a great deal of fun, especially if it sinks in that mother and father are in no mood to shorten the time no matter how loudly he shouts and screams.

Most children, when they come out for the second time, will skulk away to take stock of these dastardly new tactics being employed by their parents. It is extremely unusual for them to risk a third period of TO before they have had an opportunity to re-think their own strategy. What happens on the next occasion is crucial. It is not uncommon for parents to feel extreme guilt and remorse after the initial TO and have fundamental doubts about its ethical nature. They will probably salve their consciences and take some comfort from the improved behaviour of the child, and they will fervently hope that the lesson is learnt and that they will never have to go through it again.

The child who challenges again

Some children learn quickly that a new determination has taken over in the house and they think long and hard before they again challenge the parent's authority. Most children, however, who have been used to getting their own way all their lives, will decide merely to bide their time. Within a short while, probably no more than a day or so, they will precipitate a crisis in order to test the parents' resolve. The reaction of the parent to this new offensive is of major importance. If the behaviour continues, despite fair warning about what will happen, then the parent must *immediately* and without further explanation, take the child off to TO. If this happens, the whole TO period is likely to be over in less than ten minutes. And the next time, assuming there is a next time, will probably be over in less than five minutes. Within a very short period, intelligent children work out that the quickest way to get out of the loo is to sit quietly for the required three minutes. It is at this point that TO is serving its proper purpose – to remove the child physically from the scene of the action and allow tempers to cool. TO is the physical equivalent of counting to ten.

Explanation is essential

Time out is never done without prior explanation to the child. For a seven-year-old the explanation might go something like this:

> Arthur, Daddy and I have decided that the next time you do not do as you are told and you are naughty and lose your temper and start kicking and breaking things, we are going to take you and put you in the loo for three minutes until you calm down. After three minutes you can come out − but only if you have been quiet. If you shout or kick when you're in the loo you will have to stay in there longer. Do you understand? Let us see what three minutes feels like. Let's see if we can hold our hands above our head for three minutes. . . .

Later, when Arthur has taken in most of the message, and you have patiently gone over the bits he does not understand, you can add something like:

> So, next time you start to shout or kick, I will ask you to stop. I will remind you about having to go into the loo if you don't stop. If you carry on then I will put you in the loo. OK?

(A colleague of mine, Dr Janet Bucher, suggested an ingenious refinement that can be used to great effect, especially with children who enjoy football. If a child ignores the first request, he is shown a yellow card which has been made by the parents. A second refusal is met with a red card and a 'sending off' into TO.)

Initial misconceptions about TO

The purpose of TO is to calm, not to frighten. For this reason the child is never put in the loo in the dark. The light remains on all the time. Similarly, the child is never locked in and left. For as long as the child is in the loo, a parent remains on the other side of the door. This is the bad news, for it may mean that mum or dad has to spend 30 or 40 minutes superintending TO on the first occasion.

It is uncanny how many times this fact is used as the excuse for never using TO in the first place. Despite the logic and sequence of events – that the actual time spent in TO drops dramatically each successive time – parents sometimes latch on to the time factor as an excuse. 'I can't stand at the loo door for 30 minutes – the dinner will be ruined...I'll miss EastEnders...I've got to....' It is not uncommon for a smile of relief to come over the child's face at this point.

In the very young, TO in the loo is inappropriate since it can be done on one's knee, simply by holding the child tightly around the waist for three minutes. But no talking, since talking can be rewarding!

In the over 12s, especially when muscular boys grapple with single mums, TO is often impossible without outside help.

In homes without inside loos some therapists maintain that TO can be done by sending the child into the corner of the room. Opinions on this point differ. To have the child actually out of sight helps calm things down much sooner, especially if it means other children are not looking on, laughing, gloating, or in other ways diminishing the chances of success.

Preparing a TO room

Many doubts that parents have about TO, whether expressed openly to the therapist or not, can be allayed to a great extent by patient explanation. It is always helpful for therapists to do home visits in order to anticipate any difficulties at first hand. In Arthur's case, Caroline, a psychiatric nurse from our unit, visited the parents at home. What follows is the essence of the message she gave the parents.

> Nothing which is pleasurable must be left in a TO room. This is usually the case when the loo is chosen and *never* the case when the child's bedroom is chosen. A child's own bedroom is really the last place he should be sent as a punishment. Many children turn the tables completely on their parents by refusing to come downstairs after time is up, because they have become engrossed in some pleasurable activity, or they are just pretending to be having such a good time.
>
> Everything of interest must be removed from the loo – books, magazines, comics.
>
> Opportunities for breakage and possible injury must also be eliminated. Intelligent parents will easily anticipate what an angry child will get up to in order to increase the guilt of parents

who are anxiously listening on the other side of the door. Bleach bottles, loo brushes, spare toilet rolls – all must be taken out permanently in the anticipation that the loo will soon have to double as a TO room. This forward thinking is much better than assuming that TO will not be necessary and then being caught unprepared.

The cistern lid might easily be lifted and broken by an angry child. The solution Caroline suggested is a very simple and obvious one. Her answer was to secure the lid by the use of right-angled brackets as shown in Figure 7.1. If you think that this is going over the top then either your heart is not really in TO, or else you will draw back at the last moment when you suddenly realize that you never got around to securing the cistern lid.

You must expect a child to try and frighten you into letting him out before time is up. He might tear the wallpaper, break a window, crack the loo seat – so it is very important that nothing is left behind to help him in these ventures. The loo must become the bleakest room in the house.

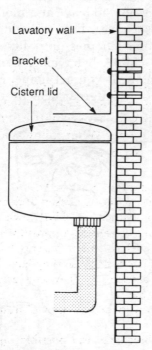

Lavatory wall

Bracket

Cistern lid

Fig 7.1 Diagram to show how right-angled brackets can make it impossible for a young child to remove cistern lid.

If a child is likely to climb out of the window then a lock must be fixed to it. Even some highly motivated parents counter this by saying: 'If you say he's bound to learn after three or four times in time out, is it really worth the effort of putting a lock on the window?' After pointing out that fixing a window lock was not a major job, Caroline left this question for the parents themselves to answer.

The key or bolt must be removed from the loo door since the child can easily reverse matters by locking himself in and refusing to open the door. In this situation, the whole thing can degenerate into parents begging the child to come out. Again the solution is easy if the problem is anticipated.

'But what happens when people want to use the loo for its proper purpose?' Is this really such an insurmountable hurdle? The child certainly hopes it is! A method can surely be worked out to tell the other members of the family when the loo is being used for its proper purpose – singing is usually the method of choice!

Unfortunately TO can rarely be done in other people's houses, and it is not always possible to leave at a moment's notice when a child starts to misbehave. The realistic answer is not to venture into other people's homes until TO on your own territory has improved a child's behaviour. Failing this, TO can always be done the moment you get home, even though things have usually calmed down a great deal by this stage.

Possible damage

Damage done by a child in TO has to be paid for. How this is done varies from house to house, but it is only fair to warn the child beforehand how the cost of any damage will be met.

If you are worried about the damage that may result from a child kicking at the door with his shoes, simply remove his shoes before you put him in. You can also empty his pockets in case he has any sharp implements with which to attack the wallpaper.

Caroline was asked a common question: 'What if the child falls ill or faints, or has a fit?' There are no absolute rules in cases like this and parents must use their own judgement. The situation may become clearer if the symptoms clear up on coming out of the loo, only to return in even greater force when he is reminded that there are two minutes of TO yet to do.

The physical strength to perform TO

TO may sound brutal and uncivilized and it is not to everyone's taste. If it is done with love and a genuine concern for the child, but with a no-nonsense air of firmness, then it is often all that is needed to turn the tide in favour of parental authority. Of course, this is no comfort to parents who are physically unequal to the task of getting an aggressive child into a TO room. Fortunately this was not the case with Arthur. There was never any doubt about dad's ability to get his son into TO, but we were less sure about mum (including mum herself). As it turned out, doubts about mum were unfounded. At the next sign of Arthur's defiance she surprised herself, sweeping him into TO before he knew what was happening.

This is how Arthur's mother put it to Caroline some weeks after the end of a successful TO schedule: 'I suddenly realized that there was going to be no end to it unless something drastic was done. I just couldn't let things go on and have him end up in care – or me in a loony bin. I knew I had to do it – and I did!' She related this with a huge smile for Caroline and a big hug for her son.

Remember that time out is the physical equivalent of counting to ten.

8
Intermittent reinforcement

This chapter is concerned with a seeming illogicality – that a child who is sometimes rewarded for good behaviour and sometimes not has a greater chance of changing his behaviour for the better than another child who is consistently rewarded.

The birth of a second child

Arnold, aged six years, was a much loved child, doted on by his parents. Although many thought that he was thoroughly spoilt, Arnold still came across as a charming and friendly little boy of whom any parent would be proud. Until, that is, his mother gave birth to Zoe. Zoe's arrival displaced Arnold from the centre of his parents' universe, and the shock to his young system was devastating.

Ever since she knew she was pregnant, mother had gone to great lengths to explain to her son what was happening. He appeared delighted and looked forward eagerly to playing with his new baby brother. Even after the birth, and the initial bewilderment that his brother was in fact a sister, Arnold continued to be very enthusiastic and insisted on visiting the hospital every day (mother was kept in longer than usual because Zoe had been born by caesarean section). Mother and father congratulated themselves on a job well done in preparing Arnold for the arrival of another child.

Dangerous behaviour emerges

The problems started soon after Zoe was brought home from the hospital. Mother had decided to breastfeed and had again explained to Arnold everything that was happening, and he appeared enthralled. Two days after her return home, with father back at work and granny out doing the shopping, mother decided to devote time to her son. They were deep into building a Lego spaceship when Zoe began to cry for food. Arnold looked briefly irritated but carried on zapping invisible aliens with noisy enthusiasm. After a minute or so Zoe's cries were becoming intrusive, and with a shrug and a smile of resignation mother got up saying, 'You've won. All my troops are dead. I'd better go and feed your sister'.

Mother went into the next room and settled down to breast-feed the baby. She did not notice Arnold come up behind her. Suddenly Arnold jumped forward and started lashing out with a plastic hammer, hitting wildly in the direction of Zoe's head. His face was bright red with anger and he shouted, 'Send her back! Send her back!'

The 'honeymoon' was over, and during the next few weeks it became abundantly clear that Arnold's jealousy of his sister was manifesting itself in an all-pervading anger. He would scream and shout whenever Zoe was being fed, he would pinch and hit her if she was sleeping, and take every opportunity to express his hatred whether he was alone with Zoe (which was virtually never) or whether an adult was in the same room. Guilt-ridden, his parents set about giving more of their attention to Arnold, but nothing they seemed to do would lessen his pleading that Zoe should be sent back where she came from. Before too long it was *Zoe's* upbringing that was beginning to suffer.

Help, before someone is killed!

Zoe was nine months old by the time the parents sought help. During that time things had got even worse and the whole household was suffering the effects of constantly high stress levels. One idea suggested was that Arnold should go off to stay at granny's for a while, but this was thought unrealistic since Arnold would be bound to see it as a rejection. And anyway granny was not getting any younger and it was felt that her health was not up to coping with a six-year-old boy. There were a million other reasons why it was a counsel of despair: it would mean a change of school, new friends, huge guilt feelings – and besides which his parents loved him too much to part with him. It was a reflection of the seriousness of the situation that they were even discussing such an option!

It fell to Alison, the senior nurse therapist to do a home visit and assess the situation at first hand. An immediate behaviour modification programme was needed even though it was perfectly clear that such an approach would do nothing for the *cause* of the behaviour, which was Arnold's intense jealousy of his sister. Such considerations had to take second place to ensuring the baby's safety. Alison also deemed it inappropriate to spend time charting a baseline since a potential tragedy could occur in the meantime. There appeared to be no special aspects about situations when the jealousy was shown; it would occur whenever Arnold and Zoe were in close proximity and would happen just as often in front of mother as in front of father. On average, the parents estimated that Arnold would try to hurt his sister four or five times a day, especially at feeding times.

Rewarding good behaviour

In a long talk with the parents Alison began to analyse the situation. The attention they were presently giving their son was, to a large extent, based on a need to keep his jealousy at bay and his thoughts away from harming his sister. Whatever mother or father was doing, they were on constant alert to detect the first signs of trouble, and would jump like scalded cats whenever Arnold made any move in Zoe's direction. It was possible that Arnold was beginning to play on his parents' fears deliberately in order to get the attention he craved. Things had reached the point that even if he was secretly beginning to accept his sister, it was not in his interests to show it. He was happy enough being rewarded (with parental attention) for acting 'bad' – Arnold was being reinforced for the very behaviour the parents were trying to eliminate.

A plan was formulated. Each parent was to be on the lookout for good behaviour and was to think of ways of rewarding it as soon as it occurred. 'Bad' behaviour, by which was meant any threatening moves towards Zoe, was, as far as possible, to be ignored unless it was obvious that action had to be taken as an emergency. Any time that Arnold went towards Zoe, something which up to now had had both parents jumping out of their seats, was to be ignored.

The rewards chosen were Smarties. Mum and Dad carried around a supply of these sweets in their pockets, and whenever Arnold was being good he was to be told what a good boy he was, hugged if possible, and given a Smartie. From now on good behaviour was to be rewarded, not bad. Arnold's parents also opted for a simple form of a token economy. They divided the day into the usual three periods, morning, afternoon and evening, and awarded a token and prize if Arnold was seen to be kind or helpful to Zoe. By this strategy contact with Zoe was actually encouraged, and Arnold would start to see that more was in it for him if he was good to his sister than if he was naughty. At the end of the day, assuming Arnold had won all three tokens, these could be traded in for an agreed reward (Arnold chose to have a bedtime story read to him by his father, which was to last for 20 minutes). It was decided that all three tokens had to be gained to win the daily prize, since if the total needed was fewer than this then Arnold might lose interest in his new-found brotherly love once he had got the necessary one or two.

Alison suggested giving the token for help with feeding Zoe. Special 'feeding' tokens, bigger, and in different colours from 'good behaviour' tokens, were made and awarded separately. It sounded a bit complicated at first, but as usually happens, a well motivated child soon gets the hang of things!

Intermittent reinforcement

Intermittent reinforcement is a ponderous way of saying that sometimes a certain behaviour is rewarded (reinforced), whilst at other times the same behaviour goes unrewarded. This might appear to be a serious flaw in the behaviour modification programme worked out for Arnold. Assuming that his parents did not have limitless supplies of Smarties, and would be reluctant to spend all their time doling out sweets, how is Arnold to know when he is going to get congratulations and a sweet for being good, and when he is going to get just congratulations? The answer is that he will not know.

This might suggest disaster, since the first time that no Smartie is forthcoming, Arnold may get angry, feel duped and revert to his bad behaviour, starting with a hefty wallop for his sister. Happily this did not happen, and to explain this apparent absurdity whereby intermittent rewards are not only as effective as continuous rewards but are, in fact, *better*, consideration must be given to pigeons. Something that happens only now and again keeps up the interest a lot longer than something that happens all the time. A pigeon in a box will keep pecking at a lever despite the fact that the vast majority of its efforts are not rewarded with seed. It is being intermittently reinforced and will keep on pecking in the hope that the very next peck will produce food.

People who play one-arm bandits are only intermittently rewarded, but that does not seem to stop them from continuing to put money into the machines. Arnold will keep being good in the hope that the Smartie will be given to him the very next time.

But when can the Smarties be cut out altogether? That is impossible to answer because all children are different. What usually happens is that gradually the 'bad' behaviour fades into the past and is replaced by more acceptable behaviour. This better behaviour then gets intermittently reinforced by less tangible rewards than Smarties – verbal expressions of love, hugging and kissing – which produce increased self-esteem in the child.

More about rewarding done 'just some of the time'

We all respond to intermittent reinforcers in real life: the hitch-hiker who thumbs a lift will continue to do so even through the majority of drivers do not stop to pick him up; the person who persists in trying to get the operator even though the line is busy knows that sooner or later the call will be answered.

It is a happy consequence that intermittent reinforcement works so well. Many parents shy away from talking about a reward system simply because they think that if the rewards are not given every time then the target behaviour is bound to start up again. A busy mother is frightened to make matters worse just because at the time her son was being good she was elbow-deep in washing or had run out of Smarties. It often takes a lot to persuade parents that rewards which are given only now and again do a great deal to keep the child's interest alive and ensure that he does not get fed-up as quickly.

But scepticism often remains. Parents ask how often they should reward, and whether they should reward immediately or only after the good behaviour has been going on for a certain time. There are no right answers to these questions and the correct spacing of rewards will have to be found by trial and error. It is best to start a programme by giving immediate rewards for good behaviour, but as this new behaviour becomes established one can try to lengthen the time before a reward is given, and finally give rewards only every second or third time that the child behaves well.

9
Stimulus control

Therapists who work in behaviour modification often talk about the ABC of behaviour. By this they mean antecedents–behaviour–consequences, which is another way of considering the events leading up to the behaviour, the behaviour itself and what consequences follow the behaviour.

Here is an example:

Mother asks John to tidy up—John refuses—mother gets angry.

The signal or stimulus—the behaviour itself—the consequence of the behaviour.

Much of the book so far has been involved with talking about particular behaviours and their possible consequences. For instance, Terry may set fires and the consequence may be that his house burns down. What leads up to the fire-setting has not been considered. Something may have prompted that particular behaviour, such as a friend daring Terry to do it. Such a dare would be the stimulus which prompted Terry's behaviour. In many situations it is possible to change a behaviour by changing the stimulus. Note the following example:

A husband has been wanting to make love all evening but his wife has been complaining how tired she feels and what a terrible day she has had. When they get to bed he makes overtures which she resists. A row develops and he goes off in a huff to sleep in the spare room.

The husband misread his wife's message (it's rather inapt to call it a stimulus!), persisted in making amorous advances (the behaviour) and paid the consequence by sleeping in the spare room.

Bad behaviour as a direct result of misunderstandings

This is a classical example of inappropriate behaviour due to misreading of signals. Either the husband picked up his wife's reluctance and was hoping to change her mind, or else the messages given out by his wife were not explicit enough and should have been a lot less subtle. Bad behaviour in children often occurs as a result of such misunderstandings. Suppose a child is told: 'Tidy up, it's nearly teatime', and instead of doing so immediately, carries on playing. It might be reasonable for parents to get angry and lose their temper. But the child's behaviour might be explained if there was scope for misunderstandings, such as:

1. If mum *usually* gave a ten minute warning of tea and did not *usually* expect things to be done immediately.
2. If the child did not know what mother meant by 'tidy up' – whether she meant clear away just his own toys or those of his brother as well.
3. If mother had not bothered to make sure that the child had heard, but merely shouted from the kitchen without waiting for a reply.

and so on.

It can be seen that ambiguous messages may well explain the bad behaviour of some children; they just do not know with sufficient clarity what is expected of them. Another common example might be the confusion a child sometimes experiences at mealtimes. If some days he is given dessert even though he has not eaten everything on his plate, and on other days he is not given dessert because he has not completely cleaned his plate, then he has good reason to be confused at his parents' inconsistency.

My child is 'schizophrenic'

Nothing is more calculated to chill a child psychiatrist's blood than when a parent says that her child must be 'schizophrenic' because 'she's such a Jekyll and Hyde character'. Quite apart from the fact that true schizophrenia is very rare in young children, it has absolutely nothing to do with the popular image of a split personality. What a parent really means is that the child behaves in a particular way in some situations or with some people, and in the opposite way in other situations or with other people. This often has less to do with the child's personality and more to do with the different stimuli given out in the different situations or by the different people involved – we are back to lack of consistency.

David is eight years old. He is known as Dave to his mother and his friends, but 'Trouble' to his father. Each parent has a completely different account of his personality – it would sound to an outsider as if they were talking about different children. Mother looks upon him as 'just a normal boy' who is naughty some of the time, but no more than anyone else of that age. Father, on the other hand, rarely has a good word to say about David, is totally frustrated by the frequency of his bad behaviour and is on the point of looking into the possibility of sending his son to a boarding school.

To the team on the unit it was immediately obvious that the side of David that Mum saw was the opposite of that which Dad saw. What became clear only after analysing the situation was that both parents were reinforcing the different behaviours in their own fashion.

David's behaviour with mother

Mother was a 'no nonsense' type of person who had been brought up in a disciplined home by loving parents. She was determined to rear her own children in the same way. Consequently she only rewarded, and then only intermittently, good and acceptable behaviour. David was given his fair share of sweets and cola but *only if he had been good*. In this way mother achieved stimulus control over her son's behaviour; when he was with her he was likely to behave well, and such good behaviour was occasionally rewarded with nice things to eat and drink.

David's behaviour with father

Father, on the other hand, gave sweets and drinks to David much more frequently than mother did, and he also gave them to him regardless of whether his son had been acting well or badly. And this was the nub of the problem. When David was with his father he would be given things irrespective of his behaviour, and consequently it was not surprising that David behaved badly much more often in his father's presence than in his mother's. Father's stimulus control worked in an indiscriminate fashion, whereas mother's encouraged acceptable behaviour.

'If you don't come in this minute I'll break your neck!'

A mother was getting increasingly desperate at her daughter's defiance. Whenever it was time for bed, Emma, who was twelve years old, would invariably be out in the street chatting to the boys. Come bedtime, mother would open the door and call out: 'Emma, it's time to come in now'. Invariably there was no response.

Much angered, mother's next trip to the door would betray her impatience. 'Emma! Will you say goodnight and come in immediately!' Nothing ever happened.

Mother's third attempt would be loud enough to wake the dead in the cemetery. 'If you don't come in this minute, I'll break your bloody neck!' Well within the minute Emma would be indoors.

Why did Emma behave as she did? Simply because it was only when mother became furious that Emma was moved to do as she was told. The stimulus in this example was not the request itself, but the volume at which it was delivered. The prescription given was that mother should bellow and scream at the first time of asking.

It worked.

There is a famous cartoon which illustrates the point. Two children are talking in the street. The girl tells the boy that his mother is calling him. The boy replies: 'Don't worry, it's only the second time'.

'Hang up your coat and hat!'

Probably the most frequent childhood behaviour complained about by adults is untidiness, especially by boys. Sometimes, as with the directive 'Tidy up', some of the confusion comes from not clearly stating exactly what the child is being expected to do. But there is no such ambiguity about 'Hang up your coat and hat'. Yet so many parental nerves are stretched to breaking point by a child's inability to grasp this simple directive.

When a child throws his coat on to the floor most parents take the child back to the hall and insist that he hangs up his clothes. But invariably the child has forgotten it by the next day. The key to this problem is stimulus control. The stimulus that an adult wants the child to react to is a verbal request for tidiness. It is often a forlorn hope.

What is needed is the substitution of a *verbal* stimulus for tidiness by a *visual* stimulus of a closing door. What is required is that the sight of the closing door should stimulate the child to hang up his coat and hat. How can this be achieved? By getting the child to put his hat and coat back on, go back out into the street, and come back in again, remembering this time that the sight of a closing door must immediately make him think of the coat rack. It usually takes very few re-runs for the new stimulus to evoke the correct result.

Must the stimulus go on and on?

Hopefully not. Let us go back to the mother who decides to get her daughter indoors by bellowing at the top of her voice at the first request. After a period of success, reinforced or rewarded by a smile of appreciation or whatever seems appropriate, her daughter will probably get the point and ask for mum to call more quietly in future. If mother agrees and Emma comes at the first time of asking, using the quieter approach, then every-thing in the garden is lovely. If Emma reverts to her old habits, so must mother.

An extreme example of stimulus control

To be the parent of twins can be represent double the pleasure, or double the trouble. Most twins have a deep emotional bond linking them to each other, but occasionally profound rivalry and jealousy get to such a frantic pitch that they constitute very real dangers. That was certainly the case with thirteen-year-old Owen and Trevor. Both boys had been fighting each other as long as their parents could remember. Sometimes it would be Owen who started it, sometimes Trevor. Each boy acted as a stimulus to bad behaviour in the other. The house was a constant battlefield and mother's health was beginning to suffer.

One day there was a near tragedy. Owen had started to tease Trevor about a girlfriend and Trevor had grabbed at a kitchen knife lying on the table and lunged at his brother. The knife cut deeply into the back of Trevor's neck and it was only swift removal to hospital that saved his life.

The parents came to the unit, bringing the boys with them. Trevor had a long scar down the right side of his neck. Mum and Dad wanted to know what to do – mum, especially, was convinced that the twins had not learnt their lesson. After initial remorse Owen had already begun to start teasing Trevor again, and Trevor was responding with his usual fury. Dad said that they had tried everything but nothing had worked. How could they ensure that one twin did not kill the other?

The solution the parents came to, in discussion with the unit staff, was bilateral stimulus control. The boys were to be separated for the foreseeable future. They were to live apart and be placed at separate schools. The relatives were aghast, as were the social services and the boys' school. In many lengthy sessions the parents remained convinced that they were doing the right thing for both boys' sakes. They refused to be swayed by mounting criticism and finally, after many months, the boys were found separate foster parents and separate schools. Visiting schedules are being worked out at present. The hope of the parents is that with advancing age will come a maturity and an ability for each boy to get along with the other – in other words, that a stimulus for dangerous rivalries might, in time, become a stimulus for cooperation and brotherly affection.

Much insight into why children behave as they do can be gleaned from an analysis of antecedents, and some behaviours are much more amenable to change by altering the stimulus that initiated them.

10
Parents rule – OK?

Many problems start small, then gradually, over a variable period, become firmly established and very difficult to alter. Many parents allow a sick child to sleep with them; this comforts the child and eases the parents' worries that something may happen during the night. And when a child is ill, it is the most natural thing in the world to keep him off school. Happily, when the child recovers, he usually goes back into his own bed, and back to school. Unfortunately this is not always the case, and sometimes the habit of climbing into the parental bed, or the habit of not going to school becomes entrenched. Of course, both these habits can happen in children who have never fallen sick, but a previous illness certainly seems to be a common antecedent.

The child in the parental bed

Whatever started the habit, whether it was illness, fear of the dark or something else, it is definitely unhealthy for a child to sleep in his parents' bed regularly. The usual pattern of events is that the child starts off in his own bed, then, after his parents are asleep, he creeps in to join them. Sometimes he sleeps on the outside next to one parent, sometimes he snuggles between the two. Sometimes, one or other of the parents wakes up, sees the child in bed, and voluntarily leaves the parental bed to get into the child's bed.

Many different reasons are given for allowing a child to remain in the parental bed. The nursing staff at the unit recently conducted a poll of the most common reasons given by parents:

1. They have tried again and again to return him to his own bed and he just keeps coming back into theirs.
2. The more they try, the more likely the other children are to wake up and cause problems.
3. If he is not allowed to stay, he starts to scream and wakes father up, and father has to get up for work.

People who have not experienced this problem have a tendency to be rather unsympathetic. To them the solution is simple: put the child back in his own bed, and keep putting him back until he gets the message. Parent power must exert itself.

The first thing is to get agreement from both parents that the habit is unhealthy and that both want the child back in his own bed. One way of doing this is for a nurse therapist to ask each parent of a four-year old child whether they think he will be sharing their bed when he is fourteen. Both parents usually look at the questioner as if she has gone mad. This is how the conversation developed between the parents and David, a psychiatric nurse:

David: Then what about when he's twelve?
Parents: Of course not!
David: Ten?
Parents: No! (At this point a note of exasperation crept in.)
David: What about eight?

Mum: I hope not! (Dad did not answer.)
David: Six?
Mum: No way!
Dad: Probably not.

Both parents agreed that it was certainly possible that the child would still be sharing their bed at five. So there was agreement that the problem was likely to go on for at least another year, and, from the look on dad's face, perhaps another three or four. Usually, at this point, both parents become very depressed at the prospect of things going on and on far into the future.

Sometimes one parent looks blithely unconcerned, and it may subsequently emerge that that particular parent is secretly quite happy with the present sleeping arrangements and really would not mind if they did not change. This is one of the reasons why parent power sometimes does not work – one of the parents wants to keep things just as they are. The reason for this reluctance to change varies but usually has something to do with the quality of the marriage, especially in regard to sexual relationships.

A marriage of equals

When the parents are at their lowest ebb, then is the time to inject some degree of hope into the situation. They are told that a frontal assault on the problem will start that very night and that the problem will be a thing of the past within two or three weeks!

The first thing to get out of the way is any thought that dad might have that this is mum's problem and nothing to do with him. It does not matter a fig that he has to get up for work at 6 a.m., the two of them are to take equal responsibility – and that means him. If he is not willing to agree to this then the whole thing is bound to fail.

With this agreement the rest of the plan is simplicity itself, and is exactly the advice they themselves would have given to a friend or a workmate who was experiencing the same problem. It can be called 'over the garden fence' advice because it is no more or less than you would expect to give to, or get from, a neighbour.

The new rule is explained to the child

First the child is told that, starting tonight, if he comes into the parents' bed then he will be taken straight back to his own room. This is explained in language that he can understand by both mother and father. He is left in no doubt that if it takes all night, and the night after that, and the night after that...then so be it. He is told that neither mum nor dad will speak to him when they take him back to his bed (thereby avoiding reinforcement by talking or cuddling), that he will be tucked into bed without a word and without a kiss, and will not be allowed a drink or a story or anything else that will draw things out. Most children appear to accept this when being told, but very few are put off from coming into the parents' bed that very night.

When the inevitable happens, and the child creeps into the parents' bedroom, he will probably pick the side of the bed occupied by the parent he considers the 'softer touch', the one who he thinks does not have what it takes to put him back in his own bed. That must be his first mistake, since whichever side he chooses, the result must be exactly the same. The rest of the night may well be a battle of wills and energy, but parents will always win if they are determined enough. It could well be that no sleep is got by anyone for the best part of a week or more, but it is most unusual for it to go on much longer. If a strict 'every other' regime is followed in returning the child to his own bed – first mum, next dad – then most children will have got the message within the week, especially if staying in their own bed is rewarded in some pleasant way the next day.

Only total change of habit will do – nothing less should be accepted. The occasional exception will be seen by a child as the start of a return to the old ways.

The problems of neighbours and the disturbed sleep of other children must not be underestimated, but neither must these considerations become the reasons why the programme is not started, or why it fails. Going to talk with the neighbours nearly always evokes much sympathy and understanding. The problem about other children is more difficult since it depends so much on the number, their ages and whether they share bedrooms. Nevertheless, a way must be found to solve the problem, and most parents are a match for even the most determined child.

The child who refuses to go to school

Children who refuse to go to school do so for many different reasons, and it is pointless to bunch them all together. Some psychiatrists say that there are two basic types of school non-attendance: truancy and school phobia. Essentially the distinction between them is: 'Do the parents know that the child is not going to school?' If the answer is no, the child is called a truant; if the answer is yes then the child is regarded as suffering from school phobia.

The typical truant is a child who sets off for school in the morning with no intention of ever actually getting there. He heads straight for town and spends all day mooching about the shops until it is safe to go home. His parents think that he is at school.

The child with school phobia is one that stays at home with the parents' full knowledge; this does not necessarily mean that the parents are happy about the absences or that they would not dearly like to see the child back at school as soon as possible. 'School-phobic' children are often thought to have more nervous and sensitive personalities than the truants, and many psychiatrists believe that they suffer from separation anxiety, i.e. that they are afraid to leave their home in case something dreadful happens when they are away.

It is often very easy to tell the two types of school refuser apart, but sometimes it is very difficult. Many 'phobic' children do *not* have obvious reasons for suffering from separation anxiety and appear to be afraid more of bullying from other children, certain teachers or lessons that they find too difficult, than worrying what may happen to mother while they are away. Truants will often say that a particular lesson or a particular teacher is the reason why they do not go to school; they claim that if they could get a fresh start in a new school everything would be all right. It rarely is. The vast majority of school transfers either fail on the first day (the child does not go to the new school either) or very soon afterwards.

What can parents do?

Many children are absent from school simply because they prefer staying at home! It often starts off with a legitimate illness which seems to go on and on. The child grows to prefer the comforts of home to the tribulations of school work. Parents are naturally reluctant to force a child to school if there is any possibility that he might be genuinely ill. The problem is that by the time the parents are convinced their child is not ill, the habit of staying home is deeply ingrained and very difficult to change.

Although the law says that a child must attend school until the age of sixteen, if a child is in his last school year and is determined not to go, there is probably not a lot anyone can do, least of all the parents, to get that child back to school. With younger children things are very different.

Errol's move to secondary school

Errol loved his primary school. At the age of eleven he moved to the local secondary school, and hated it from the first day. On that day, as a form of initiation, bigger boys threw his new school cap down the lavatory and tried to flush it away. They were caught and severely reprimanded by the year head. On the second day of the new term Errol developed a fever and was seen by his doctor. After a five-day course of antibiotics Errol seemed no better, though his fever had gone. He was given another course, but this too seemed to have no effect on the symptoms – weakness, headache and occasional sore throat. For most of the time Errol seemed not to be inconvenienced by his illness, spending most of the days building models, watching TV and occasionally helping his mother with the household chores. The doctor's visits became less and less frequent, especially when a blood test for glandular fever came back negative. The GP recommended that Errol should return to school 'to see what will happen'. Errol, after four weeks' absence, seemed to accept the doctor's advice. That was on the Friday.

On the following Monday, Errol's sore throat returned worse than ever. The doctor was called, found nothing, and suggested that Errol was naturally nervous about returning to a new school after so much absence. He recommended that the parents should ring the school and arrange for a friendly teacher to meet Errol. The advice was followed and when mother took Errol to school the next morning they were met by the form mistress and a old friend of Errol's from primary school. Errol, obviously anxious, was left by his equally anxious mother. By 11 o'clock he was back home, having walked out of school during break.

Exasperation sets in

It was at this point that all of the adults seemed to lose patience and sympathy at the same time. Father, when he came home from work, was furious. Mother felt that Errol had let her down. The GP made it quite apparent that there was nothing medically wrong, and the school began to suggest that Errol might be better placed elsewhere. The education welfare officer (the truancy officer of old) suggested a visit to our unit, where he was seen by two psychiatric nurse therapists, one male and one female, working as a team.

The assessment interview

The first interview was a very short one since only Errol and his mother came. Father, a long-distance lorry driver, was on a trip to Scotland. After talking to mother it became fairly clear that this was a problem for all the family, and that if there was to be any chance of success, father must come along too. Mum could see the sense of this but was obviously disappointed – she had been led to expect a miracle solution, which would entail Errol being taken to school each day by a member of the unit staff. This is not an unreasonable assumption and is often widely practised in some parts of the country. (Many trainee psychiatrists, psychologists and psychiatric nurses are still expected to visit homes in order to superintend children going off to school. More often than not the child vanishes out of a back window or locks himself in the bathroom and refuses to come out.)

Father was an amiable man, very worried about his son's education and at a complete loss to know what to do for the best. He said that he usually left for work long before the rest of the family got up, so that he was never around at the time when Errol was due to set off for school. On the three or four occasions when he had been around he had tried to get Errol to go to school, but this had caused such temper tantrums that father was afraid his son might have some form of epileptic fit.

It was a desperate situation which everyone agreed could not continue much longer. The advice given was what they least wanted to hear. From now on mother *and* father were to take Errol to school, starting the next morning. At this point Errol started to scream abuse and threaten to kill himself. Both parents looked totally dejected.

Here are the bare bones of the advice the nurse therapists gave:

1. Father was to take the holiday time (three weeks altogether) due to him. Father was unhappy at this suggestion but took solace from the sympathy he received from the male therapist.
2. The very next morning mother and father were to make sure that Errol was ready for school on time.
3. They were then to take their son in the car to the front gate of the school. It was decided that it was better at this stage if the parents did not go into school with Errol since that would draw attention to him. The form master was to be asked if he would see Errol in his office before lessons began. The telephone call to the teacher was made from the unit and various other points were discussed and agreed between the parents and the teacher.
4. Errol was to be told that his parents would ring the school at break, and again at lunchtime, to check that he was still there. If they found out that Errol had not made it into lessons, they were to tell him that the next day they would come into the school with their son and accompany him right up to the classroom. If the parents heard from the school that Errol had bunked off after the first lesson then he was to be in no doubt that from then on *both* parents were prepared to stay in school all day if necessary!

Errol's reaction

The atmosphere in the room became very gloomy and thick with abuse directed by Errol towards the therapists. It was very uncomfortable for all concerned because no one should underestimate the problems of going back into school after a prolonged absence – especially a new school. But sympathy can be counterproductive because things will only get worse if they go on unchecked. Errol will never go back to school from his own choice, and, hard as it may appear, it is the job of the parents to ensure that he starts back. No one else can do this job for them, and the alternative scenario of appearances in court for non-attendance, followed perhaps by various alternative forms of special educational provision, is not an option to be accepted easily.

Forward planning

It was obvious from Errol's reaction that things were not going to go easily, and therefore the parents were encouraged to put themselves in Errol's position and try to anticipate the obstacles he would attempt to erect in order to foil all our plans. In a discussion, the following points were raised and suitable strategies worked out:

1. That Errol would feign illness.
    The parents decided they would ignore this.
2. That he would refuse to get out of bed.
    He would be taken out of bed, by *both* parents.
3. That he would refuse to dress.
    Errol was to be put in the car, in his pyjamas if necessary, but would be allowed to dress in the car.
4. That he would lock himself in the bathroom.
    The lock would be removed from the bathroom door.
5. That he would run away.
    A parent would sleep with him in his bedroom, and Errol was never to be out of sight of one of his parents.
6. That he would attack his parents.
    Luckily, in this case, the parents thought that this was very unlikely, and that if Errol was aggressive they would be able to cope.
7. That Errol would threaten suicide.
    This is the most difficult, and many parents naturally falter at this hurdle. There is no answer that can come from a book. One must try to assess the danger of self-injury against the likelihood that, unless school attendance is re-established, then matters could well be taken out of the hands of the family. Neither parent thought Errol would injure himself but they resolved to be extra vigilant.

Errol, who was present throughout the discussion, gradually seemed to calm down, and appeared almost relieved. And so it was. With the wonder of hindsight we can see that Errol desperately needed to be told, with full and united parental authority, that he *was* going back to that school.

A successful outcome

The next day Errol got out of bed and dressed without protest. He was driven to school by both parents who had agreed that he could be dropped at the end of the street and not outside the school gates. Mother rang at morning break and father rung at lunchtime. Errol had remained in school and had even made a new friend. The parents insisted, as had been previously agreed, that they would both drive Errol to school for the whole of the first week, even if attendance was 100% (which it was). In the second and third weeks of father's unscheduled holidays, with tension much eased, mother and father managed to get out together and enjoy themselves. They also planned two very successful family outings at the weekend as a reward for Errol – and themselves.

Possible reasons for failure

Errol's was a success story. But not all have such happy endings. The main reason for failure is usually father's unwillingness to become involved, and that is why the presence of a sympathetic but firm male nurse therapist was so important in Errol's case. Fear of getting sacked is a very real danger, and the decision to risk unemployment to get a child back to school is one that only the parents themselves can make. It is an impertinence to do anything other than point out the long-term dangers for a child of continued school non-attendance. Other unsuccessful outcomes can be explained often by variable motivation and inconsistency. It is one thing to threaten to drag a screaming child into a car, dressed only in pyjamas, but determination must be very high for it actually to happen. In many cases the determination of the child *not* to go to school entirely eclipses the parents' determination that he *should* go.

One of the most likely causes of long-term failure is the

complacency that comes with short-term success. This success may last just as long as father's holidays, and the problem can recur the very day that Dad goes back to work. Other times when extra vigilance is necessary is the start of school after a half-term holiday. Genuine illnesses (and all children have them) can also precipitate a recurrence of non-attendance.

Single mothers of muscular teenage boys usually have the greatest problems and there is very little that one can suggest to help the situation. If the child is fifteen or over, it is unlikely that the authorities will take a very active part in getting him back to mainstream education, though they may try to arrange alternative education with work experience. If the child is much younger, then the education authority will probably have to take a more active part, but exactly what this would entail obviously varies from child to child.

The child who stops eating

The number of children who cut down on what they eat in order to lose weight is becoming an increasing problem, especially in teenage girls, although it is not rare in boys. Opinion about the best way to treat this condition is often divided, but parents are generally too ready to assume that the solution lies with the experts – they fail to appreciate that living for any length of time with a teenager who is reluctant to eat has turned *them* into the experts! A GP may only see two or three such teenagers each year, and even a physician at a hospital may not see more than about ten, unless he has taken a special interest in the problem. And it is very improbable that either of these 'experts' knows the day-to-day emotional ordeal of living with a daughter who looks as if she is an inmate of a concentration camp.

Generalizations can be misleading and children with eating problems vary greatly. Nevertheless, many parents tend to feel impotent to change their daughter's behaviour and look to others to do so for them. When a girl becomes dangerously thin it is natural to think of admission into hospital, and this is often the right thing to do. Nevertheless there is often a lack of expertise shown by hospital staff, unless they work on a specialized unit. It is a relatively simple matter to give life-saving treatment by feeding a girl intravenously, but when that girl is out of danger and convalescing, the staff of a general ward of a hospital are simply no match for the wiles of anyone determined to lose weight.

Ways of continuing to lose weight

Teenagers with eating problems become adept at appearing to eat without actually doing so. Food is deftly secreted into laps and into pockets without the nurses even being aware what is happening – though psychiatric nurses have more experience of the problems involved than their general nurse colleagues. Even when the food is actually taken into the mouth and swallowed, it is easy to induce vomiting or purging later on in order to keep the weight off. It is remarkable how many nurses and doctors are duped by an innocent-looking teenager assuring them that she has eaten all her meal. And even if some staff are vigilant and aware of the games being played, it is a small advantage when staff changes happen at the end of an eight-hour shift. Matters are compounded by the fact that, unhappily, many nurses and doctors have little sympathy with such young people, feeling that they are responsible for their own plight and that other patients have a more legitimate call upon medical time.

So where are adults to be found who care about the teenager who has an eating disorder, do not go off duty after eight hours, and are aware of the tricks that are played to avoid eating? These people are to be found, not at hospital, but at home, since they are usually the girl's own parents.

Feeding a slimming youngster

There is a fundamental difference between putting a child back into his own bed or taking a child back to school on the one hand, and forcing food into a girl's mouth on the other, and it would be morally wrong to criticize parents who are either unwilling or unable to bring themselves to force-feed a youngster. The purpose of this section is to point out to those parents who have never thought about this possibility that it has worked to good effect in some children – that is, parents can become parental again and take over the responsibility of ensuring that their daughter eats sufficient food to keep her alive.

It is one thing to agree with these sentiments in principle and quite another to have the ability to translate them into action. Books such as this cannot help very much in planning detailed strategies – they can only highlight common problems.

1. It is a problem for *both* parents and not just for mother alone.

2. Father should look into the possibility of taking prolonged leave from work.

3. Failing this, then perhaps mealtimes can be re-scheduled so that father is home to eat with the rest of the family.

4. The parents must decide, with professional help if necessary, what is an acceptable weight for their child. An agreement is usually reached that the child can only leave food uneaten or be fussy about which foods are eaten when she has been above the agreed weight for an agreed length of time.

5. Mealtimes should last as long as it takes for the girl to eat what is on her plate. Double portions may have to be given at the start of a treatment programme.

6. The whole family's cooperation should be enlisted, and all family members must keep a look-out for clandestine ways used to make food 'disappear'. This may involve a re-assessment of a parent's attitude to one child informing on another.

7. If there is a refusal to eat then the parents must consider force-feeding. Those who find this too painful to contemplate must remind themselves of the tragedy that could result from continued starvation. 'Force-feeding' is a very emotive term, but usually entails ways of ensuring that food is placed in a child's mouth and is actually swallowed.

8. The child is not allowed to go to the lavatory and lock the door. In this way the chances of secret vomiting or purging are lessened. If a child induces vomiting then another meal is immediately prepared and given to her to eat.

9. The girl is not to go out of the house unaccompanied. This will prevent her indulging in excessive exercise to burn up calories. Similarly she must sleep with her bedroom door open in order to lessen the temptation to indulge in 'jumping up and down on the spot' for hours on end.

Although it must be stressed that the advice and support of professionals are essential it will soon become apparent why parents are the real experts and the only people who care deeply enough about the well-being of their child to ensure that a tragedy is less likely to happen. It is parent power put to its ultimate test in order for a youngster not to starve herself to death. Critics who say that such an approach does nothing to get at the cause of the problem are right – but the underlying reason for the self-starvation can be probed when the child's life is out of danger.

11
Modelling and role play

All children learn some of their behaviour by modelling the behaviour of others – usually, but not necessarily, that of their parents. But modelling is not confined to children. Adults, too, are very influenced by the behaviour of others, and this is part of the reason why certain behaviours become fashionable and trendy. Before the Second World War a whole generation of men grew up lighting cigarettes for their wives and girlfriends by imitating the way Paul Heinred lit a cigarette for Bette Davis. Similarly, a later generation of film-goers shuffled around local cafés, mumbling incoherently into their chins, simply because they wanted to model themselves on Marlon Brando or James Dean. The behaviour of today's pop superstars is mimicked by millions of their fans throughout the world.

Despite the powerful influence of film stars and pop stars, the greatest influence on a child's behaviour remains the example set by his parents. It is a great source of pride for a son or a daughter to mimic or model the 'grown-up' behaviour of their father or mother. And it is greatly flattering to a parent to see behaviours copied by their children, especially when such behaviour reflects well on the parent. But, of course, bad behaviour is copied just as easily (perhaps more easily) than good. Matters are made more confusing for a child if there is a degree of hypocrisy or dual standards, such as when a child is scolded for modelling behaviour that the parents regularly indulge in themselves.

Dual standards

There are innumerable behaviours and habits which parents readily indulge in themselves but which they frown upon if modelled by their children. Swearing and smoking are two obvious examples. Many of these things are not of vital importance, and most children accept philosophically that there are things that adults do themselves which are unacceptable if done by children. Nevertheless there are children who persist in copying inappropriate adult behaviour, either openly or secretly. The first question that a parent must ask him- or herself is: 'Am I responsible for the bad habits of my child? Is he merely copying my own behaviour (or my husband's/wife's behaviour)?' It is obvious that parents stand more chance of their child losing a bad habit (or never getting the habit in the first place) if the child is not seeing that particular behaviour at home every day of his life.

Telling and showing

One of the fundamental ways a child learns is by being *told* what to do. This may sound obvious, but it is remarkable how often parents will complain of a child's behaviour without ever having explained in detail, and in language the child can understand, exactly what is expected of him. 'Tidy your room' was an example used earlier in the book. This instruction is actually very vague and can mean different things to different children. A twelve-year-old has much less reason for not knowing how to tidy a room than a three-year-old. Parents often have very unreal expectations about their child's ability to understand what he is being told. When my son was five we were always reminding him to work hard in school. It was only years later that he told us that he had taken this to mean that he had to press his pen *hard* into the paper whenever he was writing.

Many arguments between parents and children may be avoided if household rules are made clear and unambiguous. 'Tidy your room' can, after full explanation and discussion, be a parent's shorthand for 'Clear the Lego into its box, pick your clothes up off the floor, fold them and put them into your drawer. Do this *now* and don't take more than five minutes over it. Come and tell me when you have finished'. One can sympathize with those parents who cringe at such verbal precision, but they must not complain if less precise instructions are misinterpreted by a child. It also helps enormously if the same rule means the same thing to father as it does to mother!

Role playing as a means of changing behaviour

Role play is very similar to 'let's pretend' games, and it can be an excellent way of teaching a child a new behaviour or trying to change an already established behaviour. The method is best illustrated by an example.

Damien was seven years old and an only child, named after his grandfather. At home Damien was the sweetest and most helpful of children, but his behaviour in the neighbourhood and at school had earned him the name 'the omen' because of the series of films called *Omen* which starred a boy called Damien who was the son of the Devil. Calling Damien 'the omen' seemed to trigger even worse behaviour, and before long the mothers in the street were refusing to let their children play with him. Damien reacted by becoming very aggressive, especially to younger children, and a vicious circle of increasingly dangerous behaviour was set in motion. Finally the pressures brought to bear on the family became so great that they were forced to move house, change schools and even change their son's name to Toby, all in the hope of starting afresh.

It was not too long before the complaints started from the new neighbours. In utter desperation Toby was seen by a child psychiatrist who, because father was interested in amateur dramatics, suggested that the family tried role play. Since Toby was at the age when playing with girls was 'cissy', it was decided that the main characters in the role play would all be male, and that mum would act as the director. (This arrangement just happened to suit the circumstances; ordinarily there is no reason at all why females cannot play the parts of males and vice versa.) Mother decided that there should be three boys, all of the same age (which was, by no coincidence, Toby's age – seven). Toby played one boy, father played another, and grandad was roped in to play the third. The story was quite simple. Toby and father would spend five minutes playing together, each sharing everything with the other, and each having a great time. After five minutes mother would stop the role play and ask the 'boys' how things are going and how they are feeling.

Then grandad would join them and he would gang up with father against Toby, calling Toby names and trying to wreck the game.

Before grandad joined things might be represented in this way:

Father ———————— Toby

The two would be on the same level in order to represent equality (one was not bossing or bullying the other), and the thick line between them would represent a strong bond of friendship.

With the arrival of grandfather things might look more like this:

Grandfather
Father

Toby

Here Toby is represented as being in a 'one-down' position, and the bond of friendship has been broken. The alliance between father and grandfather is not one of equality (grandfather is above father and is the leader).

At this point mother can stop the role play and ask all three how they feel about the new situation and how each would choose to change things. These were the replies:

Grandad: Things are great. I'm the boss and everyone does what I tell them to, or else! We play the games I want to and I always win.

Mother: Have you any friends?

Grandad: Sure, he's my friend (pointing to father). We're good pals.

Mother: How would you like to change things?

Grandad: Things are great just as they are.

Father: I don't like it as much as before. I preferred it before he (grandad) came. We were having fun. I don't like calling him (Toby) names – it's not really fair.

Mother: So why *do* you call him names?

Father: Because he (grandad) would hit me if I didn't.

Mother: But he (grandad) says you're his friend and friends don't hit each other.

Father: He's (grandad's) not my friend! He (Toby) is. (Grandad looks surprised and hurt; Toby looks very pleased.)

Mother: How would you change things?

Father: I wish he (grandad) would go away and leave us alone.

Toby: I hate him (grandad), he's nasty. I wish he'd die.

Mother: Why do you hate him?

Toby: Because he calls me stupid and he pinched me. I hate him.

Mother: What would you like to happen now?

Toby: Dad and me to go on playing and him (grandad) to leave us alone.

How much each character was able to keep up the pretence is difficult to estimate; it was probably hardest for Toby (as shown by his reference to his friend as 'dad' at the end). Nonetheless the message was getting through to Toby about how it feels to be bullied and called names. When the role play was started all over again, this time with grandad and Toby getting on fine until father came on the scene, Toby again saw that to be picked upon and ganged up on is an unpleasant experience. It was noteworthy that on the third role play, when Toby was to be the bully, he found the part very difficult to play.

Insight into being a victim

At the end of the role play everyone had icecream and lemonade and talked about the 'game'. It was significant that Toby identified very much with his role as underdog and was able to express his feelings of unhappiness. The three adults gently took the opportunity to reinforce these ideas about the effects of bad behaviour in a group situation and it was gratifying that the lessons were not lost on Toby. Slowly Toby came to realize the effect his behaviour was having on others. He became determined to change his behaviour. He was encouraged in this by positive reinforcement for good behaviour – he was to be rewarded for playing peaceably with other children, and at the end of the week, provided there had been no complaints from the school or the neighbours, the family would plan something to do together. The parents were realistic enough to warn Toby that some children might try their best to get him into trouble, and that he was to keep his temper by walking away. The methods other children might use to get Toby into trouble, and the ways in which Toby might react to this provocation, were role played in the family and helped enormously in teaching the boy to keep his temper.

Virtually any situation can be role played and the child thereby given an invaluable insight into how it feels to be on the other end of someone else's bad behaviour. Some parents are reluctant to role play because they think it is childish and silly. For a youngster the whole exercise can be great fun at well as a powerful way of learning a new behaviour. After a while grown-ups begin to think it is fun as well!

Role play can be used in many other ways; one of the most common is teaching children the right thing to do in strange situations. Rehearsals on how to ask for things in other people's houses, how to sit your first exam and how to ring up a girl to ask her to the cinema are all ways in which role play can be invaluable. The only limitation is one's powers of imagination.

Reverse modelling

This is a reversal of the usual direction of modelling. Instead of children mimicking the behaviour of adults, adults copy the behaviour of children. It sounds a bit bizarre – and it is!

Advocates of reverse modelling as a method of behavioural modification point to its wide applicability over a huge range of activities. Almost every bad behaviour that a child indulges in can be modelled by an adult. All it takes is the guts to do it.

Showdown at Sainsbury's

A common situation is the child who throws a temper tantrum in the supermarket because he was not given a drink or a chocolate bar. Emily was just such a child – four years old, pretty as a picture but very wilful whenever she could not get what she wanted. Shopping with Emily was a nightmare, so much so that mother dreaded the thought of her daughter showing her up. Emily's tantrums had got so bad that mother had a lengthening list of shops where she felt too embarrassed ever to go again. Emily's father was no help because he had left home soon after she was born and had not been heard of since. Mother's parents were sympathetic but were really too frail to be of much help – besides which, they lived more than 50 miles away. But mum had some good friends and they were very sympathetic with her plight, although they rarely offered to look after Emily because the child's behaviour was very unmanageable, and her tempers quite explosive.

One day mum had had a particularly bad time in Boots because she had refused to buy Emily a powder puff. Mum's friend, Joan, met the two of them in the carpark behind Sainsbury's. Emily was sitting bolt upright in the back of the Mini, mum was looking completely despondent and had obviously been crying. When Joan was told what had happened she suggested that mum tried reverse modelling. Joan gave an impromptu demonstration, there and then. Putting her shopping on the bonnet of the car she started to shout at the top of her voice: 'Emily! Emily! Emily! I want a Milky Bar! I want a Milky Bar!'

Mother looked amazed and Emily looked as if she wished the ground would open up and swallow her, especially when she noticed Phyllis Williams, the girl who lived two doors away, pointing and giggling. But worse was to follow: Joan proceeded to bang noisily on the car roof, shouting and screaming even louder. It was all over in less than a minute, but to Emily it felt like an eternity.

'Poor Emily doesn't look very happy,' Joan said, grinning widely. 'I wonder why? Seriously, if I can do what I just did, and she's not even my child, then I think the answer's in your own hands.'

Mother was convinced, and had no trouble at all in convincing Emily that if there was the slightest hint of a tantrum in Sainsbury's, she would mimic everything her daughter said and did – *but would do it even louder and more extravagantly*. Emily was sufficiently cowed that she did not utter another word throughout the shopping trip. Just the *threat* of reverse modelling had brought about a miraculous change in behaviour – but, alas, not a very long-lasting one.

One week later, and after a last-minute phone call to Joan to bone up on technique, mother and daughter went again into town to do the weekly shopping. She warned Emily what would happen if there was the slightest hint of a tantrum, but it was obvious that Emily had sufficiently recovered her nerve to make a bid to regain the whip hand. Sadly for Emily, she had underestimated her mother's resolve. What happened has passed into family folklore and Sainsbury's history books.

At the check-out the familiar routine began. Emily asked for a Mars bar and mum refused. Emily asked again and mum warned what would happen if she tried a tantrum. Emily, determined on a showdown, quickly got up a head of steam and started to yell loudly: 'I want a Mars! I want a Mars!'

Mum took a deep breath, closed her eyes and said a little prayer to the effect that she hoped none of her friends were within earshot. She emitted such a high-pitched scream that the whole store stopped in amazement. Emily froze as if she had been turned into stone. Mum was determined to 'go the whole hog' and in a performance that would have done credit to Sarah Bernhardt she fell to the ground, beating her fists into a bag of ripe tomatoes.

In all, it lasted 30 seconds but the effect on Emily has lasted for the last two years. It was a watershed. Subsequently relations between mother and daughter improved significantly and although they do not always see eye to eye, Emily has never again been tempted to browbeat her mother by public tantrums.

Incidently, the manager still talks about that day, and mother has heard on the grapevine that the incident is retold again and again, always in tones of enthusiasm, never criticism.

Problems in reverse modelling

These include:

1. Lack of courage. This is the major hurdle and the one a child banks on. It is easy in theory but very difficult for some people to do in reality.
2. That it is frightening for the child. This objection can be overcome to some extent by explaining in detail beforehand exactly what you intend to do.
3. That it is humiliating for a child to witness such an adult tantrum. This is not a strong objection since most children's tempers deliberately set out to humiliate a parent into giving in – a one-off turning of the tables has a powerful logic about it.
4. That you would never have the gall to be seen in that shop again. So shop somewhere else!

Tit for tat destruction

Another brave single mother decided she had come to the end of her tether with her seven-year-old's destructive tantrums, and decided to do reverse modelling. She warned him that for everything he broke of hers, she would break something of his. He did not believe her. Peace was declared after 20 minutes of carnage. When a worried neighbour came to find out what was happening she found mother and son crying in each other's arms, surrounded by broken plates, ornaments and photographs – and a broken fishing rod, computer games, and Sony Walkman. It proved to be a turning point in their relationship.

Reverse modelling for all the family

The whole family can join in reverse modelling and it can sometimes bring about long-lasting improvement in behaviours, especially stealing and lying.

A thief in the family

Ingrid was a seven-year-old who stole indiscriminately from all members of her family. She sometimes stole quite large amounts of money, but more often she would take small items and hide them in her room. She was brought to the unit by her exasperated parents and older brother. After a full assessment Terry, a senior nurse therapist, asked to see the parents on their own. It was during this session that he suggested they might try reverse modelling. They took to it with alacrity.

Plan of action

This is an outline of the strategy that was finally agreed upon:

1. Because many of the items Ingrid stole were of absolutely no use to her at all, it was decided to connote Ingrid's thefts as a means of deriving excitement and exhilaration. In which case, all the family should join in the fun!
2. It was decided at a family meeting that the stealing was to be confined within the home.
3. Each family member was to take one item every day from every other family member. That is, Ingrid was to take something from mum, dad, and David, and they would each take one item from her.
4. A *verboten* list was drawn up of things that were *not* to be taken because they were too valuable, too essential or too dangerous in the wrong hands. Such items included school books, car keys etc. It was decided that it was OK to take money – those who did not want their money taken were to make sure that they had it well hidden.
5. There was no obligation to own up to anything that was taken, but at the end of every week all was to be revealed and all items were to be given back. A prize could be given for the most daring or the most unusual theft or whatever.

Playing dirty

Those were the official rules, but various alliances were secretly entered into in order to increase the pressure on Ingrid: mother, father and David only pretended to steal from one another – they either did not take anything at all, or else they told their victim what they had taken and where it could be found. In this devious way the real state of affairs was that Ingrid had three items taken from her each day, but the others only had one thing stolen. If you think this is too sneaky then this form of reverse modelling is not for you.

The consequence of this secret agreement was to alter the dynamics of the situation:

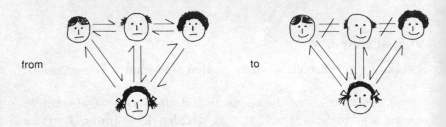

The other members of the family also pooled information on which items Ingrid would miss most. These included batteries for her Walkman and the pillows from her bed.

Mother, father and David often accused Ingrid of taking items that they had hidden themselves! When Ingrid wanted her blouse ironed urgently, mother declared that she would have gladly obliged but that someone had stolen the iron. One day there was no cooked meal because mother claimed someone had taken her saucepans!

The exchange of items planned for Sunday never came about. By Wednesday Ingrid called *pax* and said she did not like the game and wanted it to stop. Everyone feigned great disappointment, claiming that they had never had such fun in their lives, but reluctantly agreed to stop.

Another application of reverse modelling

The principle of reverse modelling can also be applied to the youngster who persistently lies. In essence, the whole family starts to lie – the more blatant the lie, the more effective. One child finally capitulated when he returned from school and was told by mum that she had prepared his favourite meal of beans, egg and chips. Imagine his chagrin when confronted by a plate of liver and spinach. Mother simply explained that she was lying – just like he did!

Conclusion

A child is likely to imitate his parents' behaviours, both good and bad, and therefore it behoves parents to make sure that they themselves are modelling behaviour that is socially acceptable.

12

Abolishing behaviour by actually encouraging it!

At first sight it may seem nonsense that a particular behaviour might be abolished by actually *encouraging* it to happen. But a little thought shows us that it can work. Consider for a moment the motives of an exhibitionist, a flasher, who gets his thrills from exposing his genitals to women. His behaviour is likely to continue the more that women are either shocked or angered by his behaviour. Now imagine instead that *every* woman he flashed at burst out laughing and begged him to do it again! This reaction would certainly confuse him greatly and the chances are that before very long he would be casting around, seeking his thrills in another direction.

It is important to look upon the example of the flasher as an illustration only. It illustrates the principle that if, instead of reacting to a behaviour with shock or anger, it is met with amusement and pleas for encores, the perpetrator will become thoroughly confused and is likely to go back to the drawing board to think of something else. The alternative behaviour that is substituted for flashing might be more or less harmful – but that is not the point and is irrelevant to the present theory. The theory states simply that if you react in the opposite way to the one which someone else expected, then there is a high probability (though, of course, not a certainty) that that particular behaviour will lose its appeal and be successfully abolished.

More examples of extinction by encouragement

A familiar example of extinction by encouragement is when a parent who discovers that his fifteen-year-old son has been having an occasional cigarette insists on the boy smoking a pack of twenty, one after the other. If stories from adult non-smokers are to be believed, this form of encouragement has sometimes had the effect of turning the teenager off smoking for life.

The same method can also be used, sometimes with very good results, with children who suddenly start to have muscle spasms or tics. The tics usually involve twitching of the muscles of the face or neck and are often made worse by a parent trying to get the child to stop. If, instead of trying to stop the tics, one actually goes out of one's way to encourage them to occur, they often diminish quite dramatically. A parent will ask the child deliberately to increase the frequency of the tics for, say, ten minutes, until his muscles actually hurt. These ten minute periods can be repeated every hour throughout each evening and all weekend. A variation on this theme, whereby *all* members of the family deliberately have a tic for ten minutes every hour, has been claimed to produce long-lasting benefits even more quickly.

One method of stopping a child from swearing is to ignore it completely. Another alternative is to take a completely opposite tack and actively encourage a child to use even fouler language at every conceivable opportunity. Let us see how it might be put into practice.

Foul language in children

The vast majority of adults look upon swearing in children as unseemly at best and positively abhorrent at worst. Even small children recognize early on in life which words are acceptable to adults and which are naughty or rude. Punishment, both verbal castigation and physical smacks, ensures that bad language is usually forced underground, to be spoken in hushed whispers when adults are out of earshot.

Of course, bad language upsets some adults more than others, and consequently some children can use expletives as a weapon against their parents much more readily than others. The whole business of bad language gets out of hand when a youngster realizes that his parents are getting very upset at the words he is using but they are quite unable to persuade him to use a more polite vocabulary. Matters often come to a head in the classic situation where a growing boy, anxious to show everyone he is becoming a man, liberally peppers his talk with four-letter words. Quite often the child is merely copying language that he hears his parents use every day. In many families mother is caught on the horns of a dilemma – she finds her husband's language objectionable but is powerless to change him, and yet she hopes to alter her son's language, even though he is only modelling himself on his father. Since this particular example is basically a no-win situation, comments will be confined to those families where both parents genuinely wish their children's language to change.

Say it again, Sam

An example of foul language in a child was seen recently in the unit. The case was seen by Barbara, a nurse therapist, and will be particularly instructive to those who think four-letter words are an exclusively male preserve. An Indian mother brought her nine-year-old daughter Samiana to the unit because the child was for ever telling mother to 'Fuck off!' at the top of her voice. This behaviour made mother extremely upset and there seemed nothing she could do to stop her daughter's foul tongue. Mother had tried bribes, threats, banishment to the bedroom, and quite hard smacks, all to no avail. Mother said that she thought Sam blamed her for her recent separation from her husband, and that the bad language was intended as a punishment by causing mother maximum anxiety and humiliation, especially in the company of relatives and neighbours. An older daughter, aged sixteen, was also acutely embarrassed by Sam's behaviour, and would no longer bring her friends home for fear of what Sam might say to them.

To look at Sam it was hard to imagine that she knew any swear words at all, let alone that she would use them. She was timid, shy and only spoke in whispers. Most of the time she spent looking at the wall and smiling coyly as Barbara tried unsuccessfully to persuade mother to give examples of her daughter's bad language (this reluctance to give examples convinced us that Sam had hit upon a very potent way of punishing her mother). Eventually Sam herself was asked what words she knew that were certain to upset her mother and sister. For a long time she said nothing. Because we had been primed by a referring letter from the GP, Barbara suggested that one of the words might be 'fuck'. Sam grinned and nodded; mother and sister looked as if they wished they were a million miles away.

Sam is asked to demonstrate

Then Sam was asked to demonstrate how she said 'fuck'. Slowly, and with much persuasion, she whispered 'fuck'. The therapist pretended she had not heard, and asked Sam to say it louder. Emboldened, Sam said it again, but still hardly above a whisper. After a few more tries Barbara managed to get Sam to say all the words in her four-letter vocabulary, at a volume that could be heard across a room. The therapist appeared disappointed and unimpressed, and asked her to shout 'fuck' as loud as she could. Mum began to look very suspicious. Try as she would, Barbara could not persuade Sam to swear louder than at conversational volume.

Finally Barbara, feigning exasperation, said that she could shout 'fuck' much louder than that, and before anyone knew what was happening, she was bellowing it out at ear-shattering decibels. Initially Sam was amused, but before long she was showing distinct signs of annoyance at such unseemly behaviour. Next the therapist suggested that Sam should go with her to meet the unit secretary and that on a signal from Barbara, Sam would say 'fuck'. Sam and Barbara went out and found Sonya.

Barbara said, 'Sonya, this is Sam, and she has something to say'. Sonya, not knowing quite what to expect, smiled and waited...and waited. Barbara kept gently nudging Sam, but she kept her mouth firmly shut. Pretending to be mildly irritated, Barbara took Sam into the street, told her that they would stop the first person who passed, that Barbara would introduce Sam, and Sam would say 'fuck'. There are no prizes for guessing what happened.

When Sam and Barbara rejoined the rest of the family it was clear that the older sister had got the point of what the therapist was trying to do, but that mother was highly sceptical about the whole procedure. Mother was told of Barbara's surprise that Sam had not sworn at people in the street, and the idea was mooted that she had not managed to swear at passers-by because she would have found it all too embarrassing. Mother was too intent on persuading Barbara that her husband was a monster to listen to these speculations. But Barbara persisted, and finally asked mother to consider if she could bring herself to call the neighbours into her house to listen the next time Sam started to swear. No matter how inconvenient, no matter what time of the day or night, as soon as Sam started to mouth obscenities, mother was to go and fetch a neighbour. This was to be done in a very matter-of-fact way, as if it were the most natural thing in the world. If the neighbours were out, mother was to wait in the street until someone passed and ask whoever it was to come in and listen.

An encouraging strategy is conceived

The plan was discussed in greater detail. The therapist pictured mother and her neighbour sitting themselves down in the kitchen, eagerly awaiting Sam's party piece. If nothing was forthcoming mother was to appear disappointed, and apologize profusely for wasting her neighbour's time. Mother was to say something like: 'I'm very sorry, Elsie, but I just wanted you to hear some really choice language. Never mind, the next time Sam's in the mood I'll come and get you. Perhaps your husband and children would like to come as well?'

The point should not be laboured. Suffice to say that it was an attempt to turn the tables on Sam by taking the shock value out of her swearing and actually *encouraging* even more bad language. Sam had chosen a way of getting at mother that was guaranteed to induce heart-stopping anxiety. If mother could only persuade her daughter that bad language was really quite amusing coming from one so young, and that Sam should swear more often in order to give everyone a good laugh, then it was possible that Sam's punishment of mother would quickly become ineffectual.

Books like this are always full of examples that worked marvellously well, with everyone living happily ever after. Unfortunately this was not the case with Sam. Mother, probably for cultural reasons, was quite unable to bring herself to do as Barbara suggested. She continued for a while to shout, smack and banish Sam to the bedroom, but now, after four months, she is beginning to talk about sending her back to India to live with the grandparents. That would be a tragedy. Other professionals are trying to help with the marital problem without success.

If you can't beat 'em...

Another way of attempting to turn the tables on a swearing child was much more successful. Christopher was ten years old and had begun to use foul language to the despair of both his parents. He was an only child and was used to getting everything he wanted. Recently he had hit upon swearing as a useful addition to his armamentarium, and would burst into a string of foul expletives to the mortification of his parents. It was clear that he would continue to use this weapon for as long as it enabled him to get his own way.

Now, generally speaking, children model themselves on the behaviour of adults; they copy the habits and manners of those grown-ups around them, especially, of course, their parents. When this family came to the unit it was decided to try reverse modelling, whereby the parents would start to copy, imitate and outdo the children. Christopher was sent out to play in the waiting room while the therapist spoke to his parents on their own. It was quickly apparent that father had reached the point where he was beginning to be afraid that he might physically harm his son.

It was first necessary to pretend that the therapist had persuaded Christopher's parents that they were being very narrow-minded and that their son's swearing was only a sign of his growing up. It was agreed that from now on they were to get Christopher to learn as many different swear words as possible, especially current ones which the parents might not know or recognize. He was then to teach his parents these new words and explain their meaning. The parents were to appear to be delighted, and to start using them themselves, especially in the company of Christopher's friends, his friends' parents, neighbours, and so on. They were to give full credit to Christopher as their teacher.

For instance, the next time that Bill's mother came to collect him from Christopher's house, mum was to psych herself up to say something like: 'It's really fascinating listening to children nowadays and all the new words. Chris taught me this one –

it'll make you laugh – arsehole – isn't it a hoot?'

In Christopher's case things never got that far. After initial bewilderment at his parents' change of attitude, and then delight in listing a string of foul words that he thought his parents had never heard (in fact they had heard every one, since foul language changes very little, from Chaucer to the present day), he finally became aghast at the idea that his mother and father were going to encourage him to use these words at every opportunity – and that they were even going to use them themselves! Something in his parents' manner persuaded him that they were not kidding and that they fully intended to implement their threat if the need arose. It never did. This story had a happy outcome and illustrates the power of the encouragement method of behaviour modification. The unit therapists tend to make use of this method a great deal and in their experience it works simply because it is what the child least expects as a reaction to his behaviour.

Parental deviousness pays off

In a very similar case a twelve-year-old boy called Martin was much more cynical and determined to test his parents' resolution. It took just one occasion to persuade him that his mother was serious. After a school football match she ostentatiously chatted, in Martin's company, to the mother of his best mate. 'So I said to her that I thought he must be a bit of a...oh, what was that word you taught me Martin? Prick! That's it! He must be a bit of a prick. Choice, isn't it? Martin calls everyone a prick. He's got such a colourful vocabulary. Martin, tell Mrs Evans some of the other words you use to describe people....' It worked like a charm and it really did not matter that Martin's mother had phoned up the day before to explain to the other woman what was going on and ask her to react in mock interest rather than shocked amazement. After all, there is a little bit of the Sarah Bernhardts in all of us!

Grandparental help by proxy

In another instance the ruse seemed not to be working, and the boy appeared to be highly amused at what was going on, especially when father brought out a tape recorder to preserve

all the obscenities his son was coming out with. At the end, when the boy had exhausted his vocabulary, father, with a huge grin, patted him on the back. 'That was tremendous! I didn't know more than about four or five of them. It's amazing how foul language changes from generation to generation. I'll play the tape to Nana and Papa and see how many words they recognize.' What father had noticed, and what frequently happens, is that even though children may have the language of the sewer in front of their parents, they are purity itself in front of grandparents. As the boy watched his father lock away the tape, and saw the look of determination in his eye, it was clear that his standing in the eyes of his grandparents was too important and it was then a simple matter to get him to persuade his father that the tape was not suitable listening for grandparents with dicky hearts.

Ten minutes every hour on the hour

Another technique which has been used to great effect is the positive encouragement of bad language for, say, ten minutes every hour, in an exactly similar way to the use of encouragement in the elimination of tics. The logic behind the idea is the same as before – that anything a parent encourages will lose its edge and finally be abandoned. The major problem is finding a credible reason to persuade the child to indulge in ten minutes of swearing. What is in it for him?

One solution to this problem is to have the child demonstrate to his parents how he is able to control his language if he wants to, in order to show them that it is not some form of addictive habit that he no longer has the power to stop, even if he wanted to (which, of course, he does not).

Something like this may be tried: 'Paul, as you know I don't like you swearing, but it looks as if you couldn't stop even if you wanted to. This doctor on the TV said that kids who swear are beginning to lose control of themselves. He said that they would find it impossible to stop'. At this point a wry smile often comes over the child's face as he begins to smell a paradox. Then comes the bit he does not expect, and cannot quite see the sense of. 'What I want you to do is to swear continuously for ten minutes – you know, really get up a head of steam – and then see if you can stop. This shrink on the box said that you may be able to stop after the first couple of goes, but that after that you'd find it more and more difficult. If that happened this bloke suggested that the parents should make an appointment with a psychiatrist.'

Temper tantrums again

This method of encouraging a particular behaviour for particular lengths of time is a useful one to consider in the case of a child with temper tantrums. For ten minutes every hour, on the hour, a child might be 'pushed', even against his will, to have a 'burst on his banjo'. Again, the trick is to find a sensible reason for such a wacky idea. One suggestion might be that temper tantrums are a good way of letting off steam and toning up the system and therefore it is most important that the techniques of screaming and thrashing around should be studied and practised – but not too much (say, ten minutes every hour). It is often very gratifying how little practice a child thinks he needs, and how soon he begins to look upon tantrum behaviour as rather silly.

Active encouragement of temper tantrums when they occur is

a very useful method of extinction. 'Shout louder, thump the floor harder, don't stop' usually have the child initially complying with parental requests, but quickly throwing in the towel as he becomes hoarse and exhausted.

Let us finish this section with the anecdote about the mother of a ten-year-old who went to collect him from a party. She was the first to arrive because the family were going on somewhere else afterwards. Brian wanted to stay at the party and set about trying to embarrass his mother into going on without him. He suddenly and predictably tried his favourite ploy. At the top of his voice he bellowed: 'Why the fuck should I?' to which his mother bellowed back: 'Because I fucking say so!' He was escorted out in a state of shock.

The problem of the neighbours

Many parents accept in principle the logic of the advice they are given, but say that they are quite unable to put it into practice. One of the commonest reasons for not actively encouraging ten minutes of temper tantrum behaviour every hour is that the neighbours would soon be battering on the wall or else reporting them to the police for child abuse. In flat-land it is very difficult to initiate any form of behaviour modification which actually encourages screaming or shouting... therapists know that, the parents know that, *and the child knows that!*

There are different types of neighbours and the approach to them is different. To those neighbours with whom the parents are at war already, it is unlikely that anything they do will please them, so they may as well get on with a behaviour modification programme for their own peace of mind.

Many neighbours are parents or grandparents themselves and are well aware of the problems of bringing up children. A direct approach is by far the best: the parents knock on their door and say something like: 'Hi, we're Garry's mum and dad. I expect that you've heard him screaming and shouting recently. Our doctor says we should not give in to him anymore. He's told us what to do but said that things will probably get worse for a while and the shouting might get louder. If you can bear with us for a little while we'd be very grateful, and Garry's behaviour will improve enormously'.

If the prospect of a face-to-face turns legs to jelly then the

gist of it can be put in a note and posted through the neighbours' letter boxes. Here is a sample:

Dear Mr and Mrs Thomas

We are your next door neighbours Cyril and Susan Edwards.
You may have heard our four-year-old son Garry! I hope the
noise hasn't bothered you too much. Because Garry has a lot of
tempers (especially when he doesn't get his own way) we decided to take him to see a doctor. The doctor has given us a lot
of advice on what to do, but he's warned us that the tempers
may get worse before they get better. This is why we're writing
you this note – if the noise gets worse in the next week or so
please have patience with us! We hope you are both well.

Yours sincerely,

Cyril and Susan Edwards

It is extremely rare for a neighbour to react badly to such
an approach. Most are very flattered and eager to be helpful,
telling stories of their own experiences or the experiences of
other members of their family. The sad thing is the number of
parents who just cannot bring themselves to talk it over with
neighbours and who then start a behaviour modification programme, only to give up early because of the constant worry
of upsetting their neighbours.

When is encouragement of a behaviour dangerous?

There is no simple answer. One can give many examples where
encouragement is not appropriate – suicidal behaviour in a
teenager, aggressive or impulsive behaviour in an overactive
child – but so much depends on the nature of the behaviour,
the personality of the child, his brothers and sisters and parents, and the inherent dangers of the situations where the
particular behaviour is enacted. All these have an influence on
the decision to suggest encouragement.

Encouragement of verbal behaviour is obviously a safe bet.
When physical behaviours are the main problem the decision to
use encouragement techniques obviously depends on the nature
of the behaviour, the age of the child and the dangers that

might occur to the child or others. Each situation is different and each must be considered carefully before a decision about encouragement is taken. The following case illustrates how dangerous physical behaviour was successfully abolished by encouragement.

A young child had got into the the habit of biting his classmates at school and this was beginning to make the other parents press for his removal. An encouragement programme was initiated and the boy was told to bite the arms of his father and mother every half-hour all through the weekend, every morning before going to school and every night after coming home from school. The biting behaviour quickly disappeared and, to everyone's relief, has not been replaced by any other.

The method has even been used for children who set fires. The child is encouraged to strike matches and light papers in a metal bin. This is done under the close supervision of an adult. The hope is that the child will learn to light fires in a responsible manner and be aware of what to do if a fire got out of control. I have grave reservations about encouragement in this situation, although I have colleagues who tell me they have used this method with young fire-setters with excellent results. I will share with you my own way of dealing with this problem. When my son was eight he started to set fires. When we discovered him striking matches under the curtains I became so incensed by the potential risk to the whole family that he was smacked across the backside until I thought my hand was going to fall off. He was then sent to bed. Half an hour later, when the full horror of what could have happened returned to haunt me, I got him out of bed and smacked him again. It was an instinctive reaction that I am not particularly proud of, but at least the house never went up in flames.

My own fire-setting as a child was not dealt with so firmly. My father reasoned with me and merely expressed the hope that I would never do such an irresponsible thing again. Two weeks later I put a candle under the toilet roll in the outside loo (the only loo we had!) and watched it go up in flames. This time my father made sure I would not be able to sit down for a week, and the memory of the indignity of being smacked across a bare bottom ensured that I developed a more responsible attitude to the safety of others!

13
Paradox

Paradoxical techniques for changing a child's behaviour are relatively new. Much about human relationships has to do with power. A child manifests his power by resisting what a parent asks or tells him to do. To some extent this is healthy and helps to develop the young person's sense of autonomy; however, too much resistance is definitely undesirable. How then can a parent harness a child's natural instincts to resist in order to achieve the outcome the adult wishes? The answer is by paradox: the parent *appears* to encourage one behaviour in order that the child resists and behaves in exactly the opposite way – the way the parent wanted all along! Some of the methods of behaviour modification discussed in the previous chapter had a paradoxical dimension to them, but the following detailed cases will better illustrate the use of paradoxical techniques.

The child who refuses to go to bed

Elizabeth is five years old. Her parents brought her to the unit with only one major complaint about her behaviour: she flatly refused to go to bed before her parents. There was never any problem in getting Elizabeth to undress, wash and brush her teeth, but as soon as bed was mentioned she would immediately go rigid and start to cry. If attempts were made to put her into bed physically, she would struggle vigorously and kick out viciously in all directions.

At first it was thought that Elizabeth was afraid of the dark and so her parents allowed her to have a night light. But this did not make the slightest difference. Friends were full of helpful suggestions, most of them concerned with parent power, i.e. becoming determined that their daughter would go to bed and stay in bed, regardless of verbal and physical protests. Unfortunately Elizabeth's parents would always give in when the noise became too loud, simply because they worried about the neighbours. Because of a long-lasting feud, the parents could not bring themselves to talk to the neighbours to tell them what they were trying to do. The only solution that seemed to work was sleeping medicine from the GP – 'drugging the poor thing up to the eyeballs', as father's mother unkindly put it.

Guilt soon put a stop to the use of sleeping draughts and the old pattern was quickly re-established; Elizabeth in pyjamas and dressing gown would settle herself down between her parents on the sofa and watch the TV until it closed down. If she fell asleep, which she usually did about 10 o'clock, no effort was made to put her into bed, because mum and dad both knew from bitter experience that the moment she was moved she would wake up and start to create a rumpus.

One friend suggested that the parents should enact a charade in which they pretended to go to bed. They would clear away the supper plates, set the table for breakfast, put out the milk bottles and be snugly tucked up in bed by 10.30. Elizabeth was quite happy to go up to bed with them at this earlier time. Unfortunately when the parents tried to go downstairs again they were rumbled by Elizabeth who insisted that she was allowed to get up and join them. Father said he had felt

infantile and it brought back memories of his childhood when a master at his boarding school caught him trying to sneak out of the dormitory after lights out.

The paradox

Elizabeth was obviously a powerful force in this family, and she exercised her power by dictating the time when she would go to bed. It was suggested by the nurse therapist that going to bed at the same time as her parents was Elizabeth's way of feeling grown-up. It did not really matter whether this was the real reason for her behaviour or not since it suited the purpose of the paradox. It was decided that from now on Elizabeth was to be *encouraged* to stay up late, in the hope that this wish of her parents would also be actively resisted (to show her independence) and she would decide not to comply, by going to bed – which was the paradoxical outcome the parents wanted.

Plans had to be made in secret in order to conceal the purpose of the paradox from Elizabeth. Consequently another appointment was made for the therapist to see the parents on their own. It was agreed that the television should be turned off and the family (mother, father and Elizabeth) would spend each evening playing board games. Immediately after supper had been cleared away they would settle down for an evening of Junior Trivial Pursuit. Now anyone who has ever played Trivial Pursuit knows that a single game can take a very long time. (Any other game, appropriate to the child's age, can be chosen as long as it takes a long time to play.) The parents must make sure that they deliberately play well or poorly in order that there is no early winner. Cheating in order to win or lose and thereby prolong the game was all part of the strategy.

The paradox is begun

Initially Elizabeth was delighted when it appeared that her parents were actually encouraging her to stay up. She readily agreed to the television being turned off in order to play a game with the grown-ups. The game started at 9 o'clock. By 11 o'clock Elizabeth was showing distinct signs of flagging interest and she was beginning not to care whether her father and mother were winning. Indeed she seemed to want them to win in order to finish the game more quickly. A number of times her father was on the brink of winning but then just could not answer one of the easiest of questions! At midnight Elizabeth was hinting that she was bored, but her parents, with simulated energy and enthusiasm, kept congratulating her for being so 'grown-up', and reminding her that other children would have given up and gone to bed long ago. Whenever Elizabeth seemed on the point of throwing in the towel her parents would praise her stamina and maturity. Whenever the game came close to being won by the parents they would fluff their question. If it looked as if Elizabeth was going to win (which it never did) the parents had decided they would demand another game to even the score.

In the wee small hours

At 1.30 mother was making signs to father that Elizabeth's eyes were closing. She gestured towards the bedrooms but father shook his head. The plan had been to go on all night if necessary. At 2 o'clock Elizabeth was beginning to get fractious and to grizzle whenever she was woken up to take her turn. She took special exception to her father tickling her to open her eyes and saying: 'Hey, you can't go to sleep on me now, I'm almost winning'. Mother, too, seemed to find fresh reserves of energy and at one stage she even splashed water lightly over Elizabeth's face. The congratulations and admiration of their daughter became even more extravagant. To Elizabeth they became even more irritating until at 2.45 she finally said that the game should finish and that everyone should go to bed. When father and mother replied that the game was at an exciting stage and that they must not give up yet, Elizabeth demonstrated her independence and power by stalking off to bed. She marched upstairs, saying that it was all silly. Father and mother, according to their plan, continued playing with exaggerated noise and enjoyment until they were sure that their daughter was soundly asleep. Luckily, and not by coincidence, it was now Saturday morning, but that did *not* mean that they could lie in. On the dot of 8 o'clock Elizabeth was called for breakfast. Wearily she came downstairs but appeared not at all interested when she was told that the game had no winner from the previous night so that it was going to be great fun to continue that evening.

Elizabeth's reluctance to start playing again was profound. Despite her parents' feigned amazement, she did not want to play into the early hours of Sunday morning. In fact all Elizabeth wanted to do was watch the television. Unfortunately the set was broken (someone had accidently removed a fuse from the plug!) and so Trivial Pursuit was brought out again. Elizabeth's heart was just not in it. She said that she would prefer to go to bed and read a book. Mother and father did not think that this was a very good idea and suggested another game – Monopoly perhaps. But Elizabeth was quite adamant – *she was going to bed.* According to the plan, both parents seemed very dubious and quite hurt that their daughter did not want to play. They decided, again according to the pre-arranged plan, that they would play the game until the early hours, pretending all the time to be having a great time, and to call up to Elizabeth every so often to come down and join them. In the event, she did not hear because she was asleep.

But she woke at about 12.30 and came downstairs for a drink. Luckily her parents were still 'playing' the game, much to Elizabeth's bemusement. Dad gave her a cuddle as mum fetched her some milk. 'Liz, love, this is so good we've decided to get rid of the TV altogether and play games every night. You're going to love it!'

Paradoxical nuts and bolts

There are some basic principles in working out paradoxical methods of changing a child's behaviour:

1. Having carefully identified the problem behaviour, it must then be paradoxically encouraged to happen.
2. A credible reason must be found by the parents for suddenly appearing to want the child to do the very thing that they had previously been wanting him to stop doing.
3. When the child shows signs of rebelling against the paradox (i.e. beginning to behave in an acceptable manner) his parents must appear very dubious about this apparent change and go out of their way to encourage his old habits.

In Elizabeth's case the problem was staying up late, and so this became the behaviour to encourage. The reason the parents gave for encouraging their daughter was the fact that she would become much more grown-up – a reason tailored to appeal to a child. When Elizabeth showed signs of rebelling against the paradox, the parents feigned disappointment and re-doubled their efforts to encourage the behaviour they secretly wished her to stop. Finally Elizabeth displayed her independence by refusing to do what her parents wished her to!

Paradox and the temper tantrum

Let us see how these principles can be applied to one of the most common behavioural problems – the temper tantrum. A paradoxical approach obviously involves actively encouraging a child to indulge in tantrum behaviour. The reason for this parental about-turn might be that it is healthy for a child to express anger in a physical way. When the child begins to have fewer tantrums (as a way of displaying his power to resist his parents' wishes), everyone is to pretend that they cannot understand why things are not working out the way they expected.

Veronica was a four-year-old daughter of a local dentist. She was the youngest of four children and the only girl. Her brothers were all in their teens, and Veronica was born long after mother had given up all hope of ever having a daughter. Veronica's birth was like the answer to a prayer. Everyone loved and spoilt Veronica, especially her brothers. If ever she was denied anything, she would immediately launch into theatrical tantrums which invariably had the desired effect – her wish was granted.

Unfortunately Veronica's behaviour fed on her tantrums and her demands became more and more outlandish. The moment of truth eventually came when the playschool teacher hinted that unless Veronica's behaviour improved she would not be welcome back in class the next term. As so often happens, bad behaviour is only seriously confronted when it spills out of the home and into the school.

The unit team decided on a paradoxical approach. The temper tantrums had to be actively encouraged. The reason given was that it was very healthy for a girl to give vent to her emotions.

Tantrums as an expression of feelings

Mother and father took a lot of time to explain to Veronica that from now on she was to have more temper tantrums because they had decided that it was good for her to show everybody how she felt about things. Starting tomorrow, Saturday, she would have to practise her tantrums so that the full force of her feelings could be seen by the rest of the family. Each hour for fifteen minutes the family would gather to watch Veronica have a tantrum and then make suggestions about how they might be altered in order to have a bigger impact. Because everyone's opinion was important it was vital that the tantrums should be witnessed by the whole family. The first tantrum would be at 10 o'clock the next morning.

On the stroke of ten the family assembled and sat around in the kitchen. Everyone was taking it all very seriously. Veronica seemed a little reluctant but was gently encouraged to get into the mood by imagining that Paul, her eldest brother, had refused to take her to the park to play on the swings. Veronica seemed amused by this suggestion but was reminded that this was all very serious and that it was vital that she should show her irritation, anger and disappointment. She did so – but in a very self-conscious and half-hearted manner. After fifteen minutes of gentle coaxing, everyone, including Veronica, contributed to a discussion on how she could be less shy and more angry the next time.

There was no next time. Veronica said that it was all very silly and refused to come into the kitchen despite pleadings from the rest of the family. Everyone, in accordance with the agreed 'script', tried to pursuade Veronica, but to no avail.

On the Sunday, Veronica started a spontaneous tantrum and was completely confused when, as if by magic, the whole family except William quickly gathered to watch, give encouragement and make helpful suggestions. It was a very poor effort on Veronica's part and lasted barely a minute. Everyone looked concerned that healthy emotions might be being suppressed. Veronica's temper tantrums never recurred, to the apparent puzzlement of her family. Veronica herself was not bothered – she had shown them that she was no one's stool pigeon!

Edward's refusal to go to school

Paradox sometimes works very quickly and with a permanent change for the better. Such was the case with Edward, a thirteen-year-old who refused to go to school. Both parents had been very distressed at their son's non-attendance but were not prepared to take him to school physically. It was the school that suggested a different tack. The plan was paradoxically to encourage Edward to stay at home for two reasons:

1. Mum would feel a lot safer with a man around the house.
2. That the school were more than happy for Edward to stay away because they thought that another school might suit

   Edward's needs better. The implication was that Edward was doing them a favour.

Monday morning came and so did breakfast in bed. Mother and father had bought a portable colour television and placed it on Edward's dressing table. It even had a remote control so that he would not have to get out of bed to change channels. Mother popped in every ten minutes or so to ask her son if there was anything he wanted. She said that she could now understand why he was not going to school – it was because he had wanted to stay at home to protect her. Edward said bluntly that that was not the reason but mother just smiled knowingly.

An open letter from the form teacher to the parents, marked 'personal and confidential' but fully intended to be read by Edward, referred obliquely to how they fully understood that a son would feel a need to protect his mother, how they felt a little sorry at the thought that they would not be seeing him again, but that smaller size classes were nonetheless welcome to a teacher. . . .

It had its effect. Edward said on the Tuesday that he had decided to go back to school, starting Wednesday. Mum looked disappointed and asked him to reconsider. She showed him the letter that she knew he had already secretly read. But her pleas were in vain and he started back the next day and took a special pleasure at the thought that the form master was mistaken when he believed he had seen the last of Edward Pike!

Considerations to be taken into account in paradoxical therapy

Paradox is not to everyone's taste, and here are some of the provisos which should be considered before such an effective behavioural modifier is put into action:

Safety

Since you are going to be encouraging bad behaviour it is imperative that the behaviour is safe. It is completely irresponsible to encourage a child in self-damaging behaviour. This is especially the case in threatened suicide. It is *not* paradox to tell a teenager who threatens suicide that if he is serious, there is really nothing you can do to stop him, but it is a dangerous paradox actively to encourage someone to try to take his own life.

Ethics

Some people object to paradox on ethical grounds. They consider it immoral to lie to a child. They especially think it is wrong to be secretly making fun of a child. The whole power of paradox is to try to give 'good' reasons why a bad behaviour should continue, and many find this contrary to their natural inclinations.

Other situations where paradox may be found useful

Sibling rivalry

So long as it is limited to verbal rather than physical battles. The paradoxical message is that the older sibling is doing the younger one a favour by helping him cope with the unfriendly people he is bound to meet in the world when he grows up. The older child might be encouraged into verbal battles to improve the vocabulary of the younger one.

Swearing

Another wonderful way of increasing vocabulary (dealt with in detail in the previous chapter).

Food fads

Telling a young child that he is much too young to enjoy certain foods and actively dissuading his mother from giving him any even to try, often works wonders. If a child is really insistent and persuades you to give him a taste of an unusual food, you must remain dubious even if he says he loves it. You must suggest that liking it at his age is *so* unusual, that he must be mistaken (*not* lying!). Paradox is even more powerful if there are other children present who *do* like that particular food.

Defiance

A child can be paradoxically encouraged to be defiant by telling him that defiance will enable him to be independently minded and to stick up for himself in a cruel world. But, of course, he must also be defiant and rude to people who are telling him to do things that he *actually wants to do*! He must refuse to come to meals even when he is hungry, refuse to go to bed even when he is fit to drop through exhaustion, refuse to say 'Thank you' even when he means it, and so on. Defiance in everything is to be encouraged and practised, and parents should appear to be very concerned and disappointed at the slightest hint of compliant behaviour.

Conclusion

Paradox is a very powerful way of altering a child's behaviour, but it is not to all parents' taste.

14

The crazier side of behaviour modification

Despite what many books may say to the contrary, even the very best plans of behaviour modifiers can fail to produce change in a child. It is all made to sound so easy with little gems like:

> John was six years old and wet his bed every night. A star chart was devised whereby John received one star for every dry night. If he won four stars he was able to buy something from the toy shop costing up to £2. In the first week he had six dry nights, and from then on never wet his bed again.

Would that all cases of behaviour modification worked as well as John's! Unfortunately, in the real world things are often not that simple, and many programmes falter despite high parental motivation and consistency – though, it must be added, poor motivation and consistency explain the vast majority of failures. The untenable fact might be that the determination of the child to remain as he is is greater than the determination of his parents to change him.

What if all else fails?

If all logical approaches to a behavioural problem fail, it is hoped that a parent may still be able to outwit a child by virtue of pure guile. These are the crazier forms of behaviour modification (assuming you did not find paradox quite bizarre!) and occupy a territory on the lunatic fringe, which more orthodox psychiatrists and psychologists rarely venture near. And yet these methods very often work where others – traditional, logic-al and worked out in the minutest detail – have failed. Within the constraints of safety and ethics, only the imagination and the courage to put them into practice limit the application of these alternative methods.

The ritual

This manoeuvre is for all would-be Laurence Oliviers and Meryl Streeps who can combine acting skill with nerves of steel and the ability to keep a straight face when doing very daft things. It may all sound very silly but its purpose is very serious.

The ritual is best suited for use by parents of children who have frequent temper tantrums or any similar sort of outburst when they do not get their own way. Instead of arguing with the child or trying to reason with him, the parent performs a ritual designed to silence him in sheer amazement, bewilder and disorientate him, and leave him completely wrong-footed.

Simon, a seven-year-old son of a single mother, has grown up used to getting his own way. His main power resides in his ability to scream at the top of his voice and make mum so worried about what the neighbours might think that she readily gives in to all his demands – a very familiar story by now to readers of this book. Whenever Simon was denied anything, or asked to do anything that did not suit him, he would start to shout. If mum did not immediately succumb, the noise rose quickly to a deafening crescendo, until Simon could be heard in the next street – literally. Mum's determination rapidly crum-bled and Simon's respect for her authority reached new lows.

But mum used to be an actress – not in the big time, of course, but she had steady bit-parts in TV soaps. Ideal qual-ities that could be put to good use in the ritual.

One day mother was preparing a meal in the kitchen when Simon came in with his friend Tony. Without a word he vaulted on to the table and reached up to the top shelf to help himself to biscuits. Mother angrily told him to get off the table and to leave the biscuits because his dinner was almost ready. Simon, showing off for the sake of Tony, told her that he would have 'as many biscuits as I want' and proceeded to cram three or four into his mouth at once. He offered a handful to Tony who diffidently backed away. Simon then proceeded to blow biscuit crumbs from his mouth, scattering them all over the kitchen. Mother demanded that he put the biscuits back immediately and tell Tony to go home for his own dinner. Simon sensed a challenge to his power and proceeded quickly to use the weapon that never failed – the tantrum. He reckoned that within seconds, as so often in the past, mother would quickly back down. When Simon was born he had had a slight fit and the word 'epilepsy' was mentioned. He had never had another fit and was not on any medication, but the doctors had given mum the idea that a severe temper might possibly bring one on. It was this fear that had made her give in so easily to her son's demands. But not this time.

At this point mother began her ritual. Without another word she stood in the middle of the room and closed her eyes. Next she stood on one leg, the other being bent back at the knee. Hopping slowly and deliberately in a wide circle, she started to buzz like a bumble-bee and then grunt like an orang-utan, flapping her arms like wings as she did so. Still hopping on one leg she then hit her forehead, first with her left palm and then with her right. Next she did a few elaborate karate-type movements, finally stood still again, and bowed low.

Both boys watched in stunned amazement as mum, as if snapping out of a trance, shook her head, said: 'Now, boys, what was I saying?' and deftly whisked the tin of biscuits from Simon's hand.

Being an actress helped mum to cast away the inhibitions that would prevent many parents from starting up a ritual in the first place. Although the effect on children varies to some extent, most react in mute surprise. When the children recover the power of speech, they often initiate the cycle all over again – just as Simon did. Mum merely began the ritual all over again. This time Simon's friend started to laugh uncontrollably and Simon began to shout at his mother to stop acting 'so stupid'. Instead of answering aggressively, mother continued the ritual to the end (it lasted about 30 seconds) and then said in a fuzzy and confused way: 'Funny that! I think I'm growing allergic to loud noises. Did I start hopping about? D'you know, it happened last week in the supermarket – this baby was screaming and screaming....' Mother's voiced trailed away since Simon was quickly making the connection for himself.

Some rules for ritual

There are a few rules which maximize the potential effect of the ritual. Firstly, it must all be done dead-pan and very seriously. But if onlookers are laughing, as Tony was, so much the better, since it serves to draw attention away from the defiant child. The ritual should not last too long or be too frightening (especially to younger children). If you are put off thinking about rituals because you think you may scare the child, it may be worth explaining in advance what might happen. But do not be tempted into a demonstration since the first time a child sees a ritual it should be 'for real' – in this way maximum impact is guaranteed. The child should be left in no doubt that the ritual is quite involuntary and is certain to happen regardless of where they are or who is present – in the street, at a friend's party, in a Wimpy, anywhere.

Rituals are potent tools and serve many functions – they take the heat out of a situation, they substitute silly actions for serious ones, and they divert attention away from the child. They also make mum or dad look ridiculous (especially a ritual which involves both parents) and most children do not relish this, especially in the company of friends. Unfortunately most parents do not relish it either, though for those of you who can bring yourself early to rituals, miraculous changes have occurred very quickly.

Here are a few tips:

1. Always try to rehearse the actions you intend to do, since spontaneity is sometimes very hard, and the effect can be ruined if you stop after 10 seconds because you cannot think of what to do next. Practice is especially important if there are two people involved – there is nothing so defeating as one parent beginning a ritual and the second one refusing to join in at the last moment.
2. Red Indian dances are the rituals chosen by most parents.
3. There is no preferred age group of children, since rituals have been known to work well over a wide age range.

Crazy eating

Many children choose mealtimes to display bad behaviour. Here is a small selection of bizarre remedies used by parents for correcting behaviours at the dinner table:

1. If a child has one favourite food, such as mashed potatoes, and refuses to try new foods, tell him that he is quite right, and henceforth serve him *only* mashed potatoes at every meal, until such time as he is begging to be allowed to eat something different.
2. In the chapter on paradox (Chapter 13) mention was made of ways of telling a child that he is just not old enough to be given a certain food because appreciation of that food only comes with age. If you are really fortunate, sibling rivalry will break out and children will virtually fight each other in their eagerness to display their maturity by eating asparagus or broccoli. The pressure can be kept up by suggesting that they are just eating it to show off, and that they could not really like it, because they are too young.
3. If a friend who is over for a meal – or better still, if a *younger* sibling – likes that food, the chances of getting a reluctant child to eat it are enormously increased.
4. If a child does not finish his meal then give it to the dog. But do not forget to give the dessert to the dog as well!

Benevolent sabotage

This is an extremely powerful method of changing a child's behaviour and is best exemplified by the teenager who never does anything for himself and expects to be waited on hand and foot. Typically he is the youngster who treats his home like a hotel. The usual reaction of parents (most often mother since she has to do most of the work around the house) to an untidy teenager is:

1. To tidy the mess up themselves.
2. To refuse ever to tidy up after them again.
3. To tidy up for them most of the time, but frequently to get angry, bitter, and resentful at the idea that they are being taken for granted.

Benevolent sabotage means that mother keeps on doing the work for her children, but with two important differences:

1. She *never* complains or criticizes the child.
2. She *always* makes a mess of everything she does.

The possibilities are endless:

1. Without the least murmur of complaint, you continue to make the bed of your fifteen-year-old son. The difference is that you do it whilst eating biscuits, making sure that crumbs are scattered between the sheets. If your son complains, *do not* get angry. Instead, apologize and promise not to be so careless in the future. When the same thing happens day after day, you must appear to be confused about the reason why, and pretend to be unable to understand why you seem to be losing your grip on things.
2. If your daughter's room is constantly untidy, continue to clear it up for her – only make sure that you put everything in the wrong place, and promptly forget where that is. Later you can 'discover' some of her most precious possessions in the wastepaper basket, and be at a complete loss to know how they got there.
3. If a child refuses to wash dishes, *do not complain*, just serve his next meal on plates that you have washed very poorly from the meal before. This is especially powerful if any of his friends are coming for a meal.
4. If a teenager is forever refusing to take adequate telephone messages for other members of the family, you still take messages for them – elaborate, detailed and invariably wrong.
5. If a girlfriend comes for a meal and your son sits like a lord expecting to be waited on, just *keep smiling* and do not let a single word of irritation escape your lips – but be sure that he gets his dessert in his lap.

The list is endless, and often produces miraculous changes in the behaviour of children and induces a new appreciation of parents.

Parental time out and reinforcements

These two ideas are merely reversals of the usual way of doing things. If a mother finds it too difficult, emotionally or physically, to put a child in time out, then she must take *herself* into time out. For four or five minutes mother retires from the fray with a newspaper or magazine and locks herself in the loo or bedroom. This procedure obviously cannot be recommended in all situations since a lot depends on what mother anticipates the reaction of her child may be – if she thinks he will react with mute astonishment then parental time out is well worth trying; if he is more likely to take advantage of her absence to destroy things or hurt himself then obviously this method is not feasible.

Parental reinforcers depend on parents giving themselves rewards for a child's continuing bad behaviour – so instead of *him* being rewarded for *good* behaviour, the *parents* are rewarded for his *bad* behaviour! Here's one way in which it has worked well:

> The parents tell the child that for each period he is good he will be rewarded by a star or token, but each time he is bad, not only will he not get the star or token, but the parents will award themselves 25p out of his savings account (or a similar sum out of their own money, though this is generally less painful to the child). When the parents have £2 they will then go out and buy a bottle of wine (say) and ostentatiously enjoy it in the child's company, thanking him fulsomely for enabling them to have such a good time. At the end of the week, assuming there is enough money in the kitty, i.e. assuming the child has been bad enough, the parents are to arrange a babysitter and finance an evening out, being sure constantly to thank the person who made it all possible. Most children, kind-hearted as they are deep down, rebel at being the provider of parental largesse. And yet the only way to stop this unseemly parental self-indulgence at their expense is to behave better. . . .

Parental self-help groups

If all else fails the only thing left is to advertise in the local papers for other parents of badly behaved children and start a self-help group. The group could hire a church hall once a week and exchange horror stories about their offspring. There could be a league table for the worst behaved child and his parents could win a prize. Parents could role play situations and discuss strategies.

Further reading

It is not my intention to give an exhaustive list of books dealing with behaviour modification in children. The following titles are intended only as a guide to further reading.

For an introduction to behaviour development I would recommend *Child Development* by A. Christine Harris (West, 1986).

For more advanced treatises on behaviour modification in children and young people readers should consult *The Practice of Behaviour Therapy* by J. Wolpe (Pergamon 1973), *Cognitive Behaviour Modification* by D. Meichenbaum (Plenum, 1977), and *Children and Behaviour Therapy* by A. Graziano (Aldine, 1984). Also recommended is *Treating Children's Fears and Phobias: A Behavioural Approach* by R. Morris and T. Kratochwill (Pergamon, 1983).

Another useful book is *Behavioural Treatment of Problem Children: A Practical Manual* by Martin Herbert (Academic Press, 1980).

For those readers intrigued by the more unconventional approaches alluded to in this book, may I suggest they consult and enjoy *Change: Principles of Problem Formation and Problem Resolution* by P. Watzlawick, J. Weakland and R. Fisch (Norton, 1974).

Index

Learning
Resource Centre
Stockton
Riverside College